AF260865

Devour:

Art & Lit Canada

is dedicated to the Canadian voice.

ISSN 2561-1321
Issue 014

Devour
Art & Lit Canada

Find some of Canada's
finest authors, photographers and artists
featured in every issue.

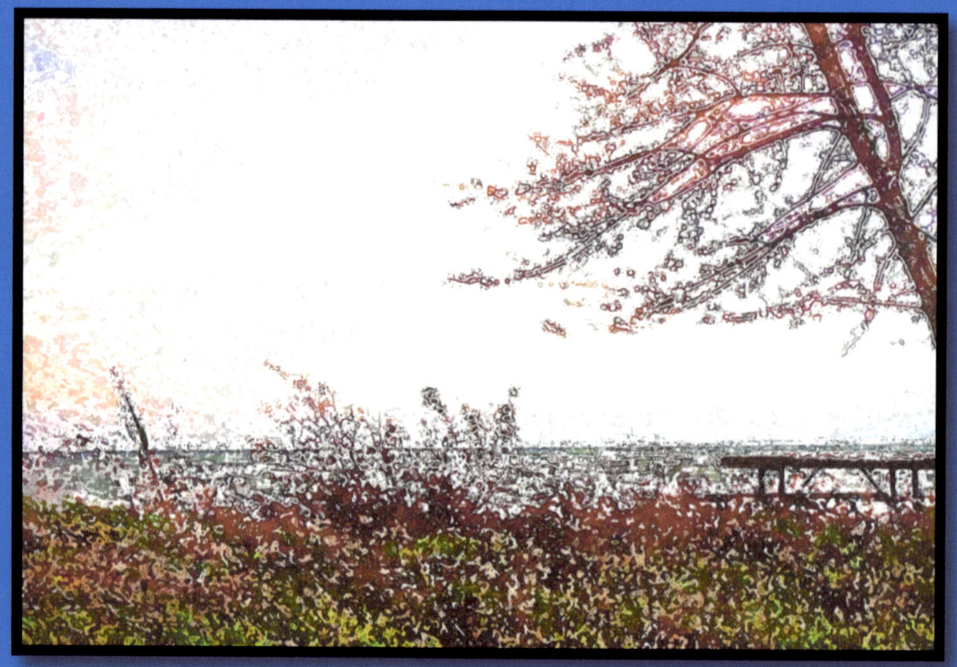

Presqu'ile Provincial Park
Richard Marvin Tiberius Grove

The mission of *Devour:*
Art and Lit Canada
is to promote Canadian culture by
bringing world-wide readers some of the best
Canadian literature, art and photography.

ISSN 2561-1321
Issue 014
Fall 2022

Devour: Art and Lit Canada

5 Greystone Walk Drive
Unit 408
Toronto, Ontario
M1K 5J5

DevourArtAndLitCanada@gmail.com

Cover Photograph – Richard M. Grove

Editor-in-Chief – Richard M. Grove
Layout and Design – Richard M. Grove

Welcome to this 14th issue of Devour: Art & Lit Canada. This is a special issue featuring three of Canada's finest poets: bpNichol, Don Gutteridge and Laurence Hutchman. Stay tuned for our regulare winter issue where we will continue to bring our world-wide readers some of Canada's most talented writers, poets and photographers.

See you between the pages.
Richard Grove otherwise know to friends as Tai

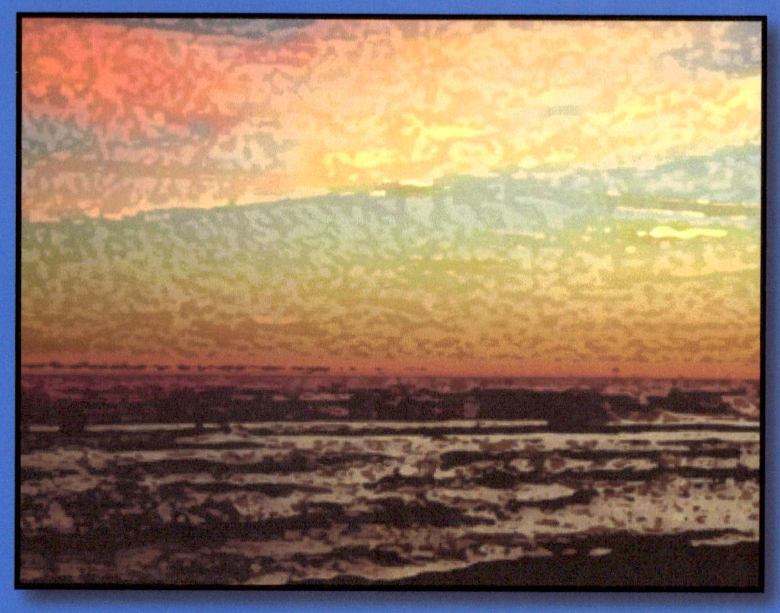

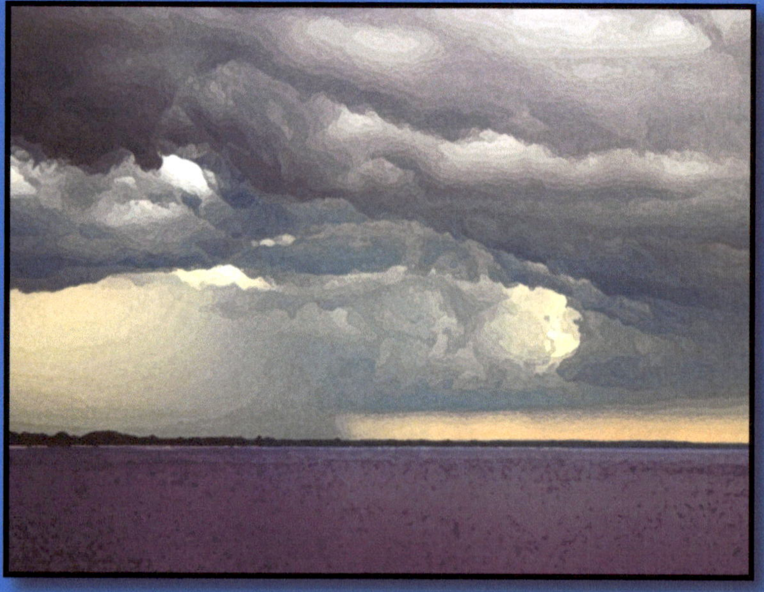

Presqu'ile Provincial Park
Richard Marvin Tiberius Grove

Devour
Art and Lit Canada

Content

Features:

www.WetInkBooks.com

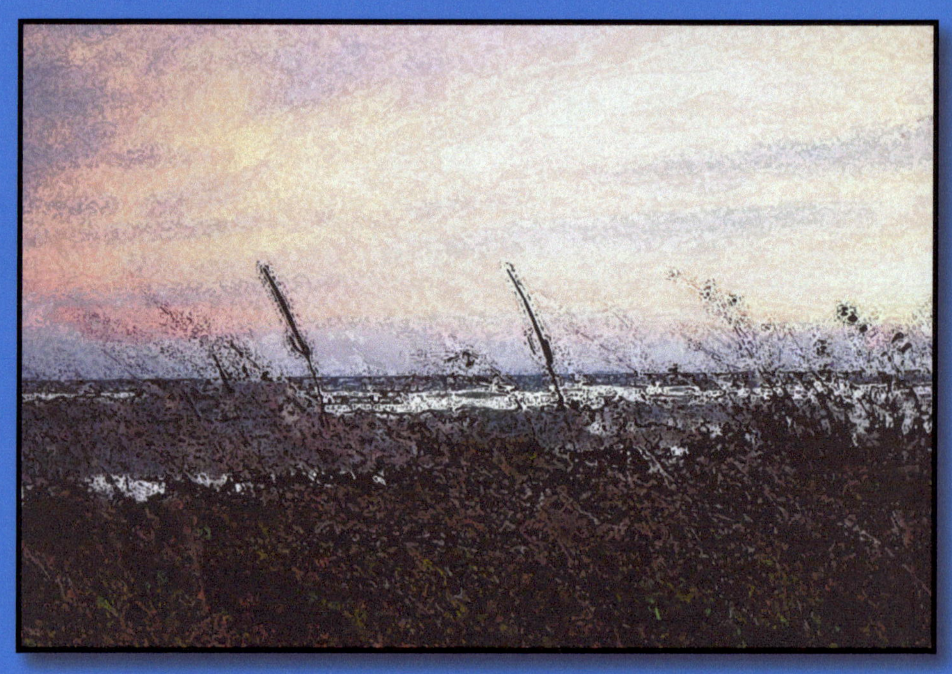

Richard Marvin Tiberius Grove

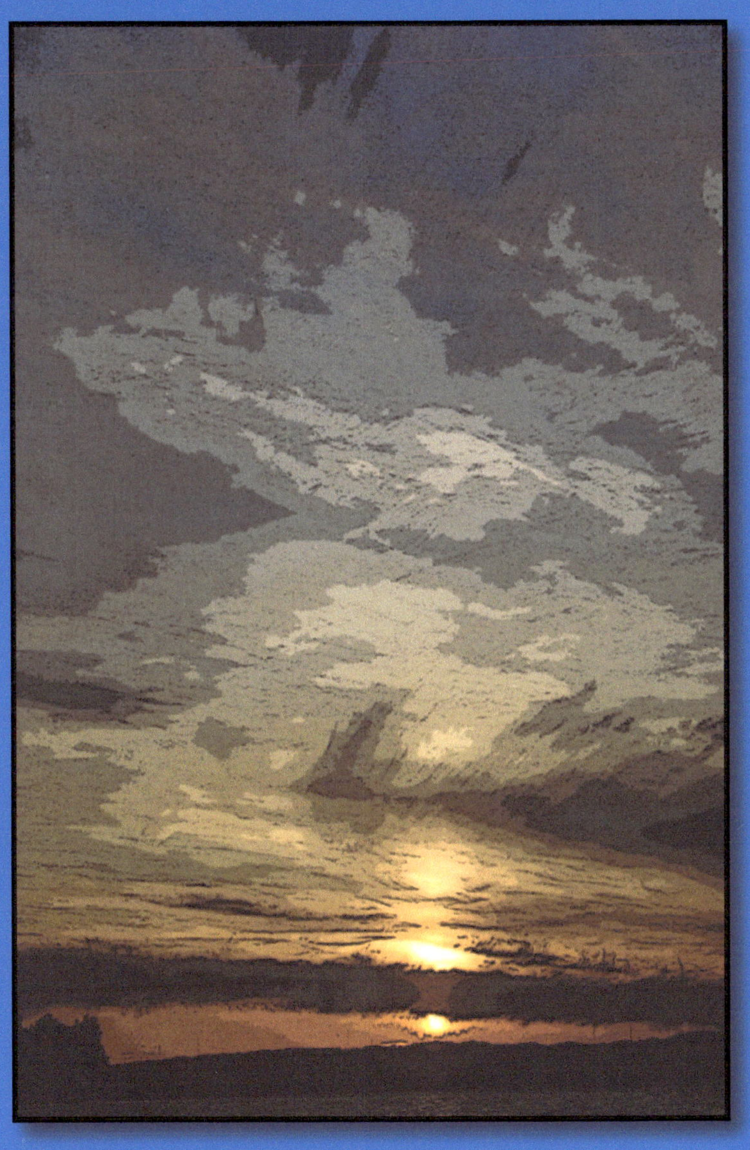

Richard Marvin Tiberius Grove

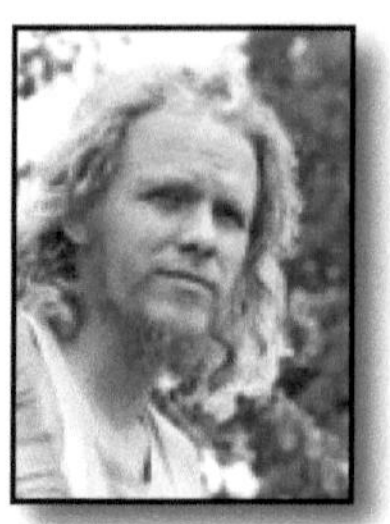

bpNichol: A Recollection

It is nearly impossible to put a label on the extensive work of bpNichol, work that consists of lyric poetry, sound poems, screenplays, concrete poems, visual gags, jokes, fiction, depiction, computer poems, drawings, songs, graphic narratives (what he called "nary-a-tiff"), cartoons, linescapes, and just about anything that involved human sounds, textuality and the alphabet. He was, if I were to put a label on him as an artist, a Renaissance Man. Not only was he experimental in his ground-breaking approaches to breaking lines, he was also madly innovative, a surrealist as much as a Dadaist, bending language, text and all of its components. A poem of his can be just one word, such as:

em ty

or a ten-book oeuvre, such as *The Martyrology*, a massive work in progress cut short by his untimely death, or a prose-booklet, *The True Eventual Story of Billy the Kid*, which, along with three other works of his that year, won the Governor-General's Award in 1970. His accomplishments and bibliography were vast and varied.

He died young. On the operating table. He was only 44. He suffered from chronic and debilitating back pain. In 1994, a street in Toronto was named in his honour, *bpNichol Lane*, the alley behind Coach House Press where he was one of its first editors. He was a member of the sound poetry quartet known as *The Four Horsemen*, a forerunner in some ways to what we know today as spoken word. He wrote for the highly successful children's television show, *Fraggle Rock*, created by Jim Henson. He was a contributing editor at *Open Letter*, an influential literary magazine of the 70s and 80s. The human imagination was his ecosystem, the impulse to create his *modus operandi*.

This is what novelist and poet, Michael Ondaatje, wrote about him:

In all of his work and life, wherever you stood within it, you were aware of the two pulls of song and alphabet which had been bound together into the rock of literature centuries ago. He knew that chaotic noises made up the song at the far end of the ballroom. Puns and howls allowed him a short cut across the dance floor… He hovered somewhere between Fred Astaire and Hugo Ball [founder of the Dada movement].

I was reminded of my relationship with the work of bpNichol when recently I viewed his computer poems, *First Screening,* on Poetry Daily's Newsletter for November 29, 2021. Douglas Lurman's comment on this work also makes it clear how innovative and relevant bpNichol's writing remains to this day. You can view the poems and read the commentary at this link: https://poems.com/poem/first-screening/?utm_source=PD+General+Email+Newsletter+List&utm_campaign=e7c67ba767-PD_NL_DONALD_REVELL_2020_03_31_COPY_01&utm_medium=email&utm_term=0_b494a3846d-e7c67ba767-44702871#featured-poet

My recollection/poem that follows is dedicated to the memory of Beeper, aka, bpNichol, an early influence of mine who gave me license as a poet to experiment and play.

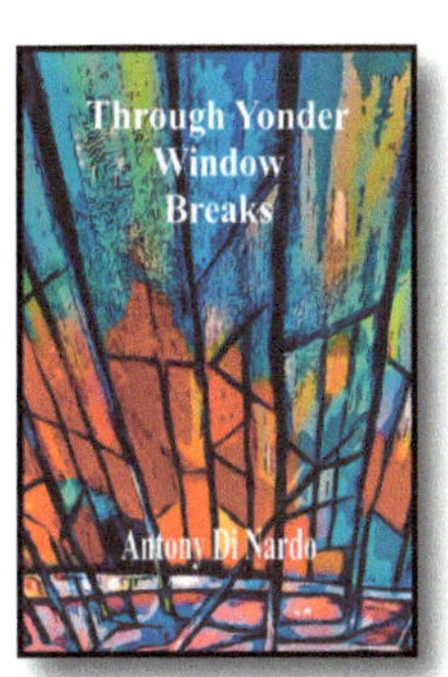

Article by
Antony Di Nardo
Prize winning poet
dinardoa@me.com
https://www.wetinkbooks.com/antony-di-nardo/

Here is another link to bpNichol –
https://poetryinvoice.ca/read/poems/two-words-wedding

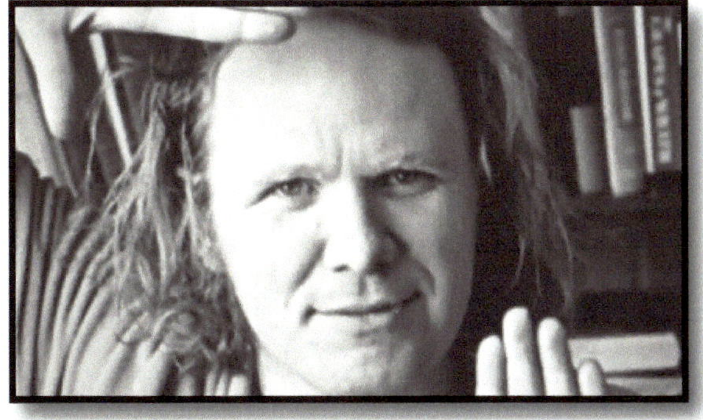

Beeper (A Recollection in Three Tenses and Five Parts)
by
Antony Di Nardo

I

History begins in 1974
at Lakehead University
on the stage of a lecture hall,
The Four Horsemen, Beeper
among them, playing with
the alphabet, syncopating
to the thrill of syllables,
performing in sync, in
discords and harmonies,
Beeper, a tower and a conduit,
tongue and cheek,
grunts and gutturals,
what language's like
when stripped down raw
and naked, his face, his hair
on fire as I listen, reconstructing
the spoken sounds
I put to spoken lines
stamped across the screen
in my 24-year old head

II

I never see him again.
Beeper dies in 1988,
some say a victim of his therapies,
the chronic burden of his back,
some blamed the surgery.
Blocks and blocks
of concrete poems
lay stacked upon the tracks
he left behind for others
to take the alphabet in hand
and send it on by coach
or cybernetics
to readers in the future

III

We find common ground,
a past and future tense, back
in 2005 when Grain
Vol. 32 No. 3 features
the Christmas cards of bpNichol
(they're not what you think),
15 pages collected
under the title *Some Scapes*,
minimal text, contra-
dictions, black on white,
white on black,
birds and linescapes,
handmade letters,
waves that weave
into something else entirely
and the poem that follows
on page 101 is mine,
Skaters in Bruegel's
"The Hunters in the Snow",
another sonnet capped
"with snow that hasn't left for ages"
and as calculated
as any word or letter placed
on the marquee of a page

IV

The future ends in 2021
in the present tense when I view
Beeper's *First Screening*,
a moving diorama of
coded poetics, 13 poems,
words and letters scrolling
on a screen, composed in 1984
on an Apple II, without sound
nor syntax, the pixels
of his imagination programmed
to render gray matter
into light, the medium
into media, shifting, surging,
scuttling crab-wise
across the screen, a
visual, restless stamp
of language hard at play

V

Beeper, the poet
ghost of writings past,
of present and to come,
the needle in a haystack,
the singular in signifying,
a-typical in type,
rituals of his visuals
coded in every word
that makes a sound,
his poem
A / Lake / A / Lane / A / Line / A / Lone
carved in concrete
down the alley that leads,
like any poem,
to somewhere else

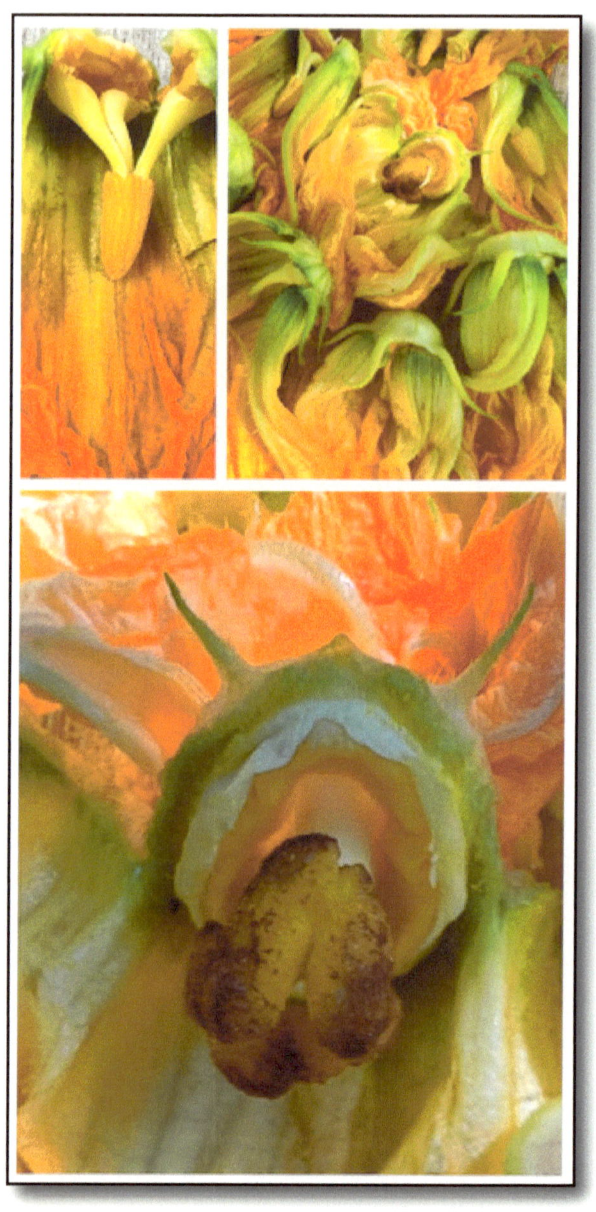

Ann Di Nardo

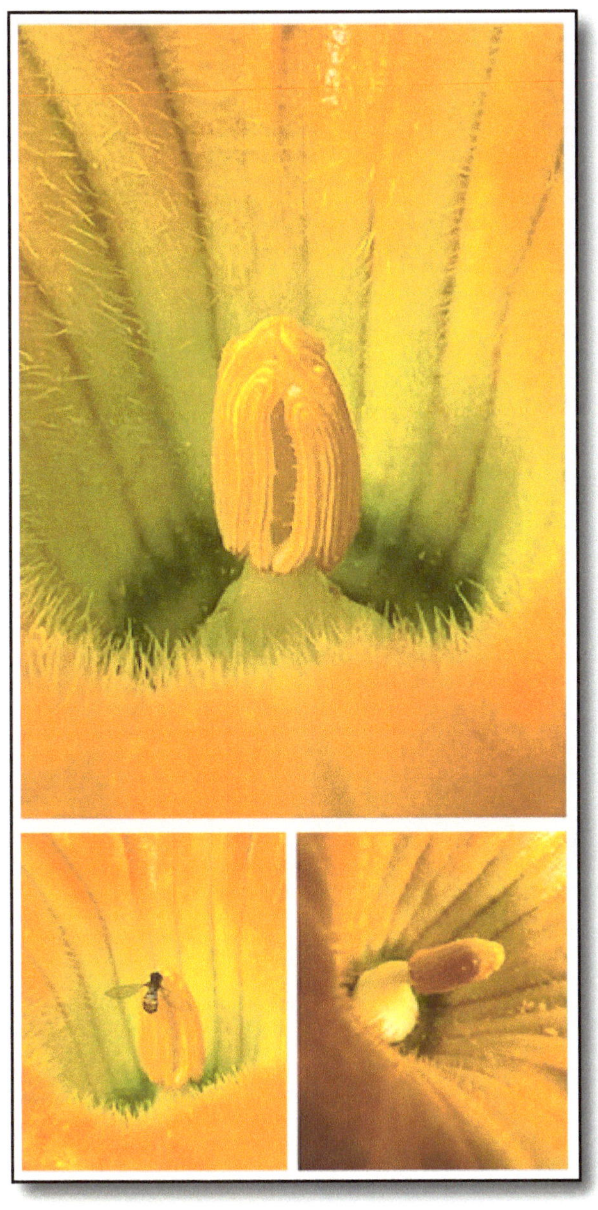

Ann Di Nardo

Don Gutteridge

A Biography by Kimberley Grove

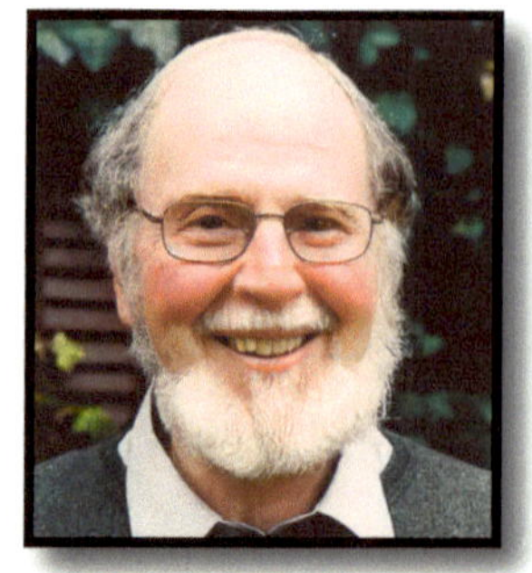

Don Gutteridge started his writing career when he was confined to his bed for nine months with rheumatic fever when he should have been enjoying Grade 2. Don was never lazy so he read enough books to fill his imagination and learn the craft of writing. When he returned to school in Grade 3 he wrote a story for his teacher Miss McDonald. She praised it so much that he realized he was on to something. And he has been writing ever since.

He has published 45 poetry books, 13 novels, 12 mysteries and 11 non-fiction books, as well as numerous articles. In his own words he talks about the thrill of his first published poem in a respected literary magazine, The Fiddlehead. "In the Fall of 1960, my wife Anne and I, both starting to teach that month in the Elmira High School, and decided to live in the nearby village of Elora. We moved into the servants' quarters of the old George Drew homestead and began our married life. I now made a life-changing decision. Having had poems published in Western's literary magazine, I decided I would start sending the few new short lyrics I was writing to The Fiddlehead poetry magazine, edited by Professor Fred Cogswell. Tucking several poems into my case, I walked to the local post office (there was no mail delivery in the village) and, both thrilled and fearful, I mailed the poems to be judged, not by student editors, but by some literary man or woman of taste, 2000 miles away. Every morning for two months, I walked into the village square to check my mail. I watched the leaves go gold and crimson and finally fall and drift. There was no response to my maiden gambit. I felt crestfallen and began to regret announcing to Anne that I was planning to become a published poet. Sometime in the chill of November, there was a letter for me, my own self-addressed envelope. I let it sit on the kitchen table awhile and, when Anne was abroad, found the courage to open it. One of my poems had been accepted, a six-line fragment I had been debating sending, but with it a short note in Professor Cogswell's scrawl, to say the poem would be published in the Spring edition of the magazine. I was a published poet on my first try. And thus began a fifty-year relationship with Fred Cogswell, a luminary of our literary world. Within three years, he would publish three of the mid-length narrative poems I had begun to write and, in 1968, my first published book, Riel. I was no longer an apprentice. That Autumn of 1960 was one of the seminal experiences of my life." The Riel book was such a masterpiece that CBC picked up on the genius of the writing and did a radio drama of it.

For the rest of this 6,000 word bio you can find it in: 978-1989786574 – *The Canadian Poet Who Wrote Himself Whole* — *See below for url.*

<h1 align="center">All Don Gutteridge books
published by Hidden Brook Press and Wet Ink Books</h1>

2016 – 9781927725405 – Title: *Inundations*
https://www.amazon.ca/s?k=9781927725405&crid=1820Y0P7EKW2P&sprefix=9781927725405+%2Caps%2C234&ref=nb_sb_noss

2018 – 9781927725580 – Title: *Home Ground*
https://www.amazon.ca/s?k=9781927725580&crid=1VO8EUFOMRGWC&sprefix=9781927725580+%2Caps%2C258&ref=nb_sb_noss

2019 – 9781927725702 – Title: *Out of the Blue*
https://www.amazon.com/s?k=9781927725702&crid=3RR5NW1W1XCNQ&sprefix=9781927725702%2Caps%2C92&ref=nb_sb_noss

2019 – 9781927725863 – Title: *Village Dreaming*
https://www.amazon.ca/s?k=9781927725863&crid=27H234A7QW03T&sprefix=9781927725863+%2Caps%2C93&ref=nb_sb_noss

2019 – 9781927725696 – Title: *Inking the World*
https://www.amazon.ca/s?k=9781927725696&crid=1D7N7V8WL3JNJ&sprefix=9781927725696%2Caps%2C288&ref=nb_sb_noss

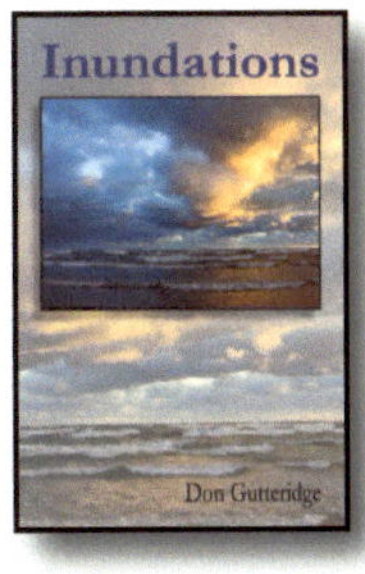
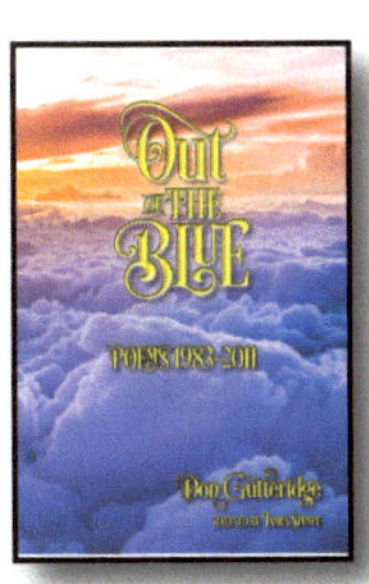
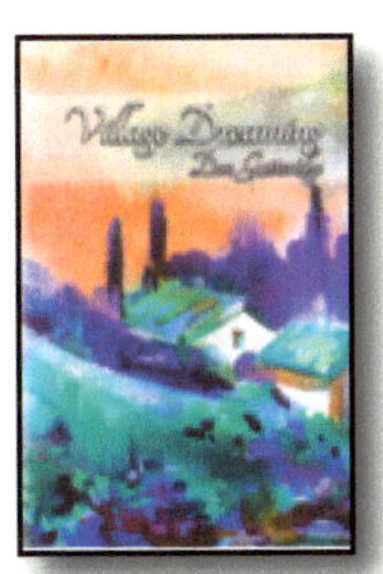
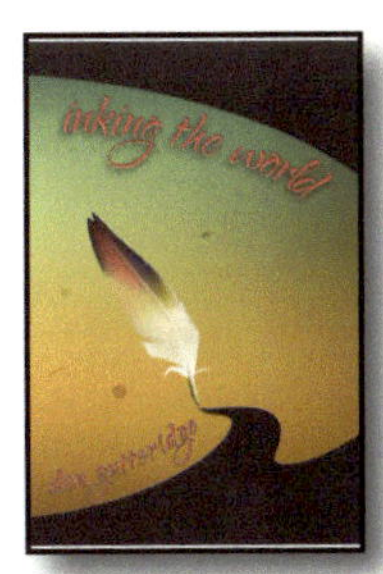

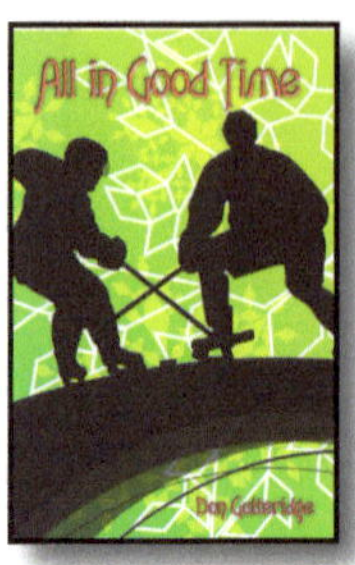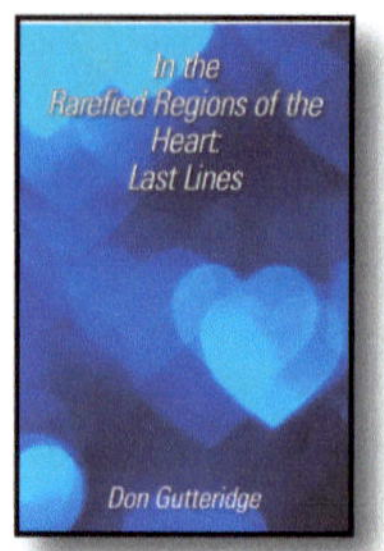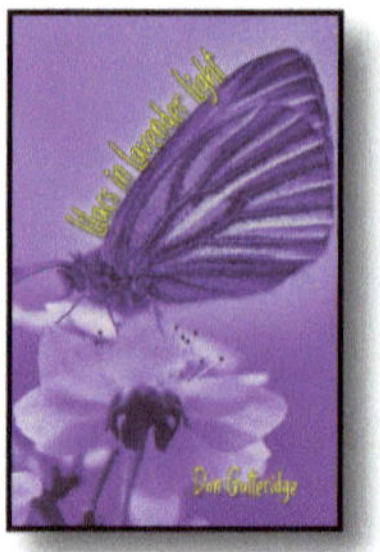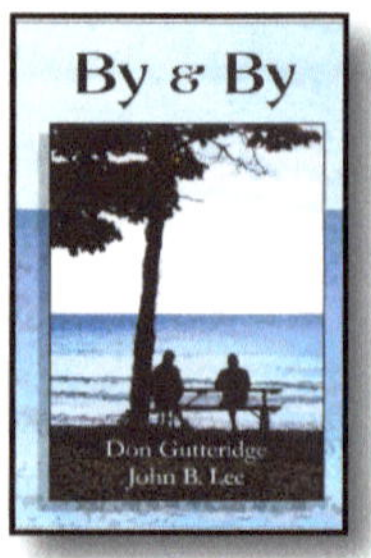

2020 – 9781927725726 – Title - *Point Taken: Collected Poems 2014-2020*

https://www.amazon.ca/s?k=9781927725726&crid=2X9NFWJ9ZJYK2&sprefix=9781927725726+%2Caps%2C114&ref=nb_sb_noss

2020 – 9781927725986 – Title: *In the Rarefied Regions of the Heart*

https://www.amazon.com/s?k=9781927725986&crid=2X2DPYSSX5RN5&sprefix=9781927725986%2Caps%2C131&ref=nb_sb_noss

2020 – 9781989786062 – Title: *Lilacs in Lavender Light*

https://www.amazon.ca/s?k=9781989786062&crid=22A72UPH4QOUB&sprefix=9781989786062%2Caps%2C77&ref=nb_sb_noss

2020 – 9781927725955 – Title: *All in Good Time*

https://www.amazon.ca/s?k=9781927725955&crid=XMO1DBJZ3EX2&sprefix=9781927725955+%2Caps%2C252&ref=nb_sb_noss

2020 – 9781989786109 – Title: *By & By*
– Authors: Don Gutteridge and John B. Lee

https://www.amazon.ca/s?k=9781989786109&crid=11TAI3OXJWANH&sprefix=9781989786109%2Caps%2C80&ref=nb_sb_noss

2020 – 9781989786161 – Title: *The Derelict Heart*

https://www.amazon.ca/s?k=9781989786161&crid=332HTKJH1U81F&sprefix=9781989786161%2Caps%2C76&ref=nb_sb_noss

2020 – 9781989786222 – Title: *Hearthbeat: Poems of Family and Home-town* – **Editor:** Don Gutteridge

https://www.amazon.ca/s?k=9781989786222&crid=3PM5J60PRJQ3X&sprefix=9781989786222+%2Caps%2C74&ref=nb_sb_noss

2020 – 9781989786246 – Title: *Invincible Ink*

https://www.amazon.ca/Invincible-Ink-Don-Gutteridge/dp/1989786243/ref=sr_1_1?keywords=9781989786246&qid=1661549214&sr=8-1

2021 – 9781989786314 – Title: *Into the Milkweed Meadow*

https://www.amazon.ca/s?k=9781989786314&crid=34KVN7R4MDFKD&sprefix=9781989786314+%2Caps%2C96&ref=nb_sb_noss

2021 – 9781989786390 – Title: *Where Rivers Run Deep*

https://www.amazon.com/s?k=9781989786390&crid=2DITIVNP622BJ&sprefix=9781989786390+%2Caps%2C98&ref=nb_sb_noss

2021 – 9781989786413 – Title: *More Boding than Blood*

https://www.amazon.ca/s?k=9781989786413&crid=8YGZES1MTIK8&sprefix=9781989786413+%2Caps%2C93&ref=nb_sb_noss

2021 – 9781989786529 – Title: *The Ardent Dark*

https://www.amazon.ca/s?k=9781989786529&crid=11S8ZP05ULX36&sprefix=9781989786529+%2Caps%2C95&ref=nb_sb_noss

2021 – 9781989786598 – Title: *Ploughing the Home Ground*
https://www.amazon.ca/s?k=9781989786598&crid=H0EG2CVFP4ZW&sprefix=9781989786598+%2Caps%2C94&ref=nb_sb_noss

2022 – 9781989786512 – Title: *Masters of the Craft 1st Edition*
https://www.amazon.ca/s?k=9781989786512&crid=CMSGVG4RO1Q2&sprefix=9781989786512+%2Caps%2C100&ref=nb_sb_noss

2022 – 9781989786611 – Title: *Going for the Grail*

https://www.amazon.ca/s?k=9781989786611&crid=2VGGLLPYJX7U7&sprefix=9781989786611+%2Caps%2C100&ref=nb_sb_noss

2022 – 9781989786628 – Title: *Lover's Moon*

https://www.amazon.ca/s?k=9781989786628&crid=3RPNU94V4QXM5&sprefix=9781989786628+%2Caps%2C72&ref=nb_sb_noss

2022 – 9781989786635 – Title: *The Home We Never Leave*

https://www.amazon.ca/s?k=9781989786635&crid=2GKN8RJPLV8HM&sprefix=9781989786635+%2Caps%2C80&ref=nb_sb_noss

2022 – 9781989786703 – Title: *Death at Quebec*

https://www.amazon.ca/s?k=9781989786703&crid=A1DVAA734HV2&sprefix=9781989786703+%2Caps%2C79&ref=nb_sb_noss

2022 – 9781989786734 – Title: *Trawling for Truth*

https://www.amazon.ca/s?k=9781989786734&crid=159NP21CUFWPC&sprefix=9781989786734+%2Caps%2C82&ref=nb_sb_noss

2022 – 9781989786758 – Title: *Kingdom Come*
https://www.amazon.ca/Kingdom-Come-other-poems-
Gutteridge/dp/1989786758/ref=sr_1_1?keywords=9781989786758&qid=1661735545&sr=8-1

2022 – 9781989786765 – Title: *A Goat Footed Dance*
Coming Soon - Check Amazon with the ISBN and the title.

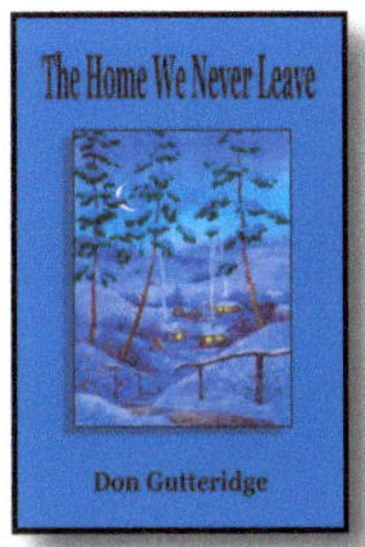
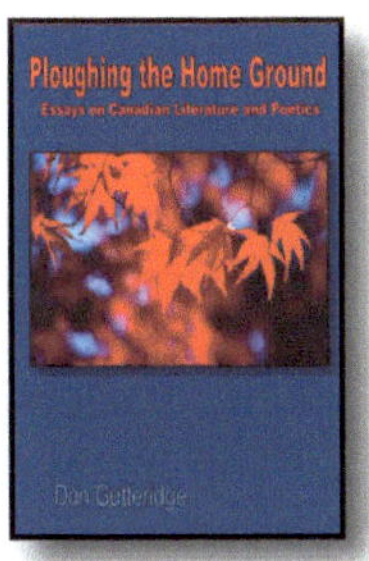
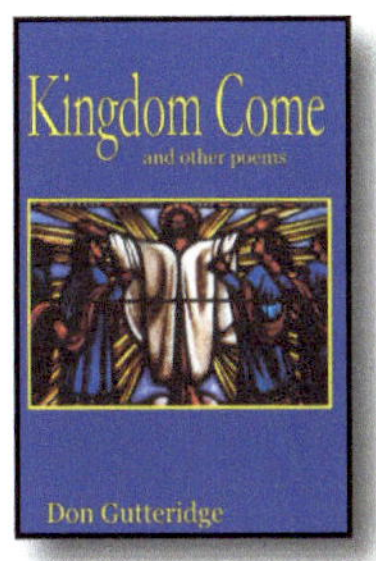
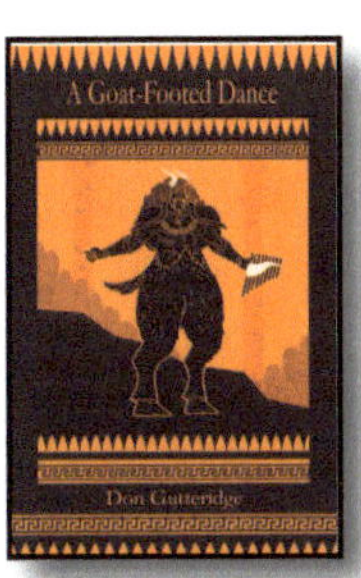

2022 – Click here for a **free** on line eBook that includes 3 of Don's poems starting on page 218 – *Framed and Familiar* – Editor – Antony Di Nardo

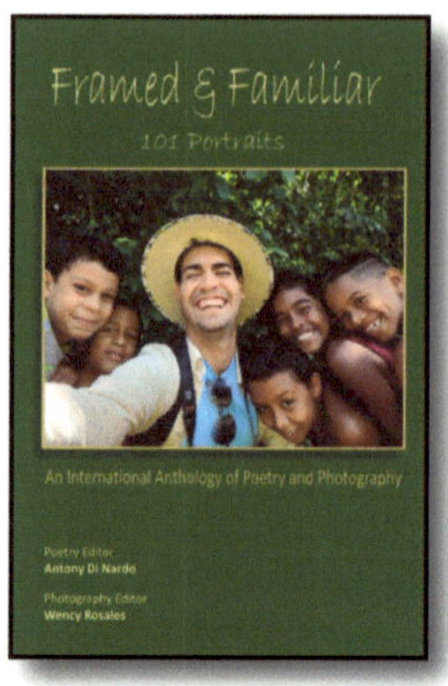

Books about Don Gutteridge:

– 978-1989786574 – *The Canadian Poet Who Wrote Himself Whole: Revealing the Poetics of Don Gutteridge*
– Author: Miguel Ángel Olivé Iglesias

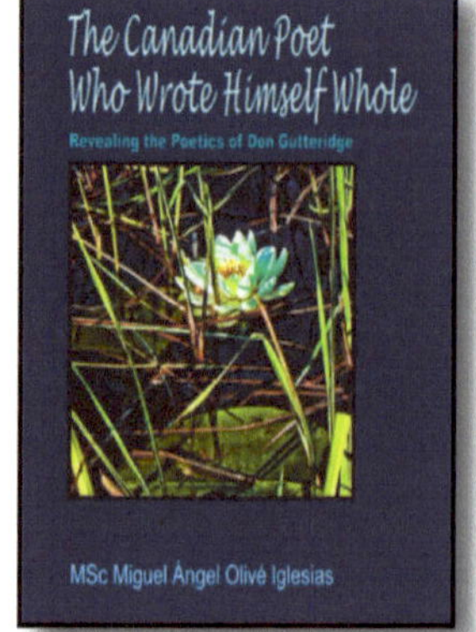

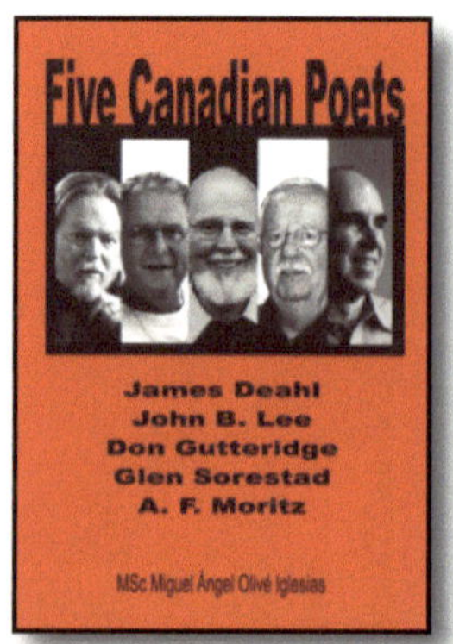

– 978-1989786369 – *Five Canadian Poets: Analytical Essays on, James Deahl, John B. Lee, Don Gutteridge, Glen Sorestad, A. F. Moritz* – Author: Miguel Ángel Olivé Iglesias

Please note that the prices of Don's books on Amazon and other eStores are all over the map. Some prices are high and some are low. Some are on sale and some are not. Sometimes they have free shipping and sometimes they do not. We have no control over the retail price. All we can do is provide a suggested retail price via my distributor.

Point Taken (Hidden Brook Press, 2019), a huge, 600 page, 7 X 10 inch, welcome undertaking, puts together most of Gutteridge's previous work. I must say that those early years in his life when he was "consuming the small library there (at Point Edward and nearby township) and writing both his first poem and his only play", were such a strong influence for his career, and a reminder of my own childhood.

Those were actually career-defining moments: "… he spent his first eleven years in a childhood enlivened by schoolyard chums and summers spent sunning on Canatara beach and paddling in the chill waters of Lake Huron… pristine days of his boyhood… There he spent three idyllic years… " that furnished Don's budding formative period and left marks on what would be his exceptional style and ability to recreate the past and lay it down freshly, strikingly and kindheartedly. It also built a foundation for his gallant, brave and confident attitude towards today and his being at peace with tomorrow.

This book has the rare touch to make me travel. While on my spatial-temporal voyage, I have been led into my own soul, my own memories, dusting many of them out of an almost forgotten past. I thank Gutteridge for it.

It unveiled gently, completely, a universe of shimmering words and images to replenish the soul. Jack Magnus tells us of Don's craft "in making his images sing…"

The book is divided into self-standing yet mutually-cohesive titles and dates that feel like sections, hand-guiding the reader across its over seven hundred pages. Despite its length, Gutteridge has succeeded in collecting poems that will stay with us long after we have finished the book. John B. Lee tells us about Gutteridge and his poetry: "we might carry these poems with us where we go…" We will put the book down with a mixture of states and feelings wafting about us. We will feel a bit of fatigue from the long, edifying journey, but also a generous pinch of satisfaction for being witnesses to the extensive high-polish oeuvre the author has compiled throughout his prolific writing career, magnificently displayed here. We will be proud for sharing in the message and scope of his work, sincere acknowledgement to the merits of the book and the poet, and a sense of belonging to that group of people who are now in possession of an extraordinary volume.

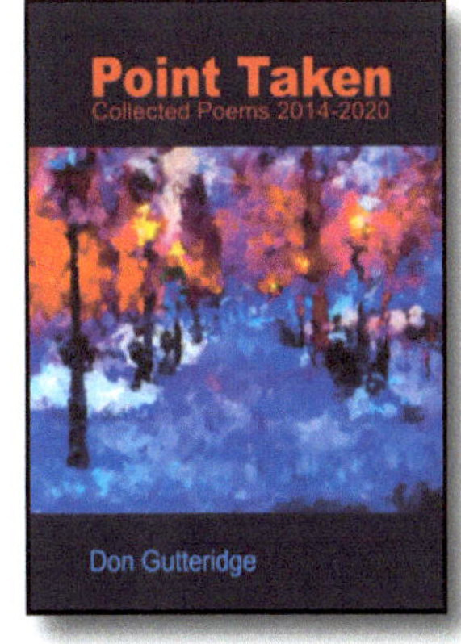

Excerpt from: *The Canadian Poet Who Wrote Himself Whole* by Miguel Ángel Olivé Iglesias

Interview with Laurence Hutchman by Janet Fraser

JF: Your book *In the Writers' Words* illustrates your deep passion for and knowledge of Canadian modernist poetry. As far back as the nineteen-seventies, you studied modern and contemporary Canadian poetry. The thesis of your 1988 doctorate from the Université de Montréal is titled "Style into Vision in Three Canadian Poets: Margaret Avison, Al Purdy, and John Newlove". Your mission in your recent book *In the Writers' Words* has been to gather and bring to the forefront poets crucial to the development of a national literature and in danger of 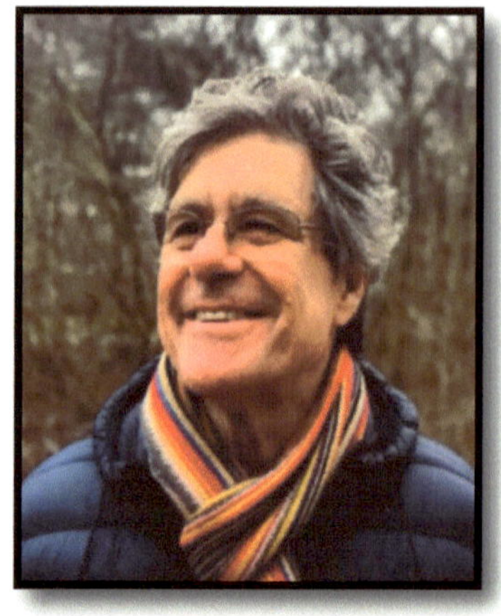 being forgotten. Since you completed your interviews, the majority of which took place in the 1990s, all eight poets have died. Speak about the legacy of these poets. Are there other poets you would have liked to have interviewed and included in this book? If so, who and why?

LH: I think the modernist poets broke new literary ground and helped to take Canadian poetry in a wholly different direction away from a formal classical style toward more open form. Irving Layton, for example, who was influenced by American writers, explored new avenues of expression, by developing his own passionate individual voice speaking about love, sex, and politics. He was, of course, an iconoclastic poet. It was so important to have a poet like him writing during this time because he was able to bring the spotlight on poetry in Canada and to help gain a larger audience. Louis Dudek, influenced by Pound, was more interested in poetry of ideas, and wrote longer poems *Europe, En México* and *Atlantis* which are fascinating because of their controlled structure, varied tones, and development of their ideas. As a man of letters, he brought some vigorous thinking and aesthetics to Canadian poetry having spent number of years in New York even serving as a secretary for Ezra Pound. He encouraged a kind of objective poetry. Al Purdy who began to write seriously after 1960 when he travelled to Montreal to associate with the writers in the 1950s and then finally settling down in Prince Edward County, where he learned how to write about the land in such an individual way: he found the hidden code, the underlying substratum, the almost concealed history through his own idiosyncratic exploration of his place. When you go to Prince Edward County, you run into Al Purdy poems here and there. Raymond Souster on the other hand introduced us to the life in the city, expressing the living scenes of Toronto. P.K. Page drew on many sources. Her poems were structured, formal, elegant, and powerful. She was influenced by A.M. Klein, Patrick Anderson, and F.R. Scott. In my opinion these ones represented some of the best writers of the time. There were writers that I would like to have interviewed such as Irving Layton, Leonard Cohen, Margaret Avison, John Newlove and Michael Ondaatje. They changed Canadian poetry in elemental way during the mid-century period.

JF: In March 2012 you attended a centenary birthday party for the late Irving Layton at the University of New Brunswick Saint John, which was part of Layton parties, which took place throughout Canada. I was impressed that you made a long-distance return day trip without complaint, in fact with graceful enthusiasm, and that you presented a paper on Layton written for the event, and that you read your wonderful poem "Lust", written in homage to Layton. Talk about your personal and literary relationship with Irving Layton.

LH: The first poetry reading that I attended as a student was at the University of Western Ontario in 1967 and featured Irving Layton and Earl Birney. It was a great place to begin. The previous year I had discovered Layton's "The Birth of Tragedy" in a high school anthology which made an immediate impression on me. I loved the individual phrases, "Love, power, huzza of battle," "yet a poem includes them like a pool," and the last lines, "while someone from afar off / blows birthday candles for the world." This drew me to his great book of poetry *A Red Carpet for the Sun*. I met Irving Layton several times. The last time in the late nineteen eighties was on Somerled Avenue in Montreal where we talked about the state of contemporary poetry. I recently wrote a poem based on his reading, which was published in my book, *Personal Encounters*.

JF: Modernist Canadian poets, including you, have been influenced by earlier poets as well as their contemporaries. In your precision and in your detailed descriptive passages leading into myth I am reminded of Keats. In your colloquial discourse, your vivid realism, and your mastery of free verse, I'm reminded of Wallace Stevens and William Carlos Williams. Williams famously said, "No ideas but in things", yet with you there is the sometimes startling juxtaposition of broad metaphor. Please comment on your poetry development, what got you started and kept you going. Can you make a kind of mission statement, or artist's statement, about your work?

LH: I've always been fascinated with language, rhythm, and rhyme. In Ireland, when I was two or three my father brought nursery rhymes to life. I remember he would read Rupert Bear comics from *The Daily Mail*.

Accompanying the pictures were writing, a prose part and poetry. There was a story and then there were poetry lines, couplets. I remember the excitement of hearing the words rhyme, the music of the rhyme. My interest in reading poetry developed in public school when we had to memorize of poems, Archibald Lampman, Bliss Carman, E. J. Pratt, and others. John Keats was an early influence, especially in high school with the "Ode on Grecian Urn" and "Ode to Autumn" which I thought was a perfect poem. This poem impressed me because I saw it as a kind of cinematographic development from stanza to stanza and his evolving tone in the poem created such a poignant effect in which the form is so integrated with the subject. And the texture of his language, the way that he could use poetic devices of synaesthesia etc. At this time, I was also drawn to T.S. Eliot, W.B. Yeats, and D.H. Lawrence. Poetry was like a puzzle, and I enjoyed taking the pieces apart and analyzing them in the context of the poem.

My high school classmate, Rolf Harvey who was living down the street, introduced to me the poems of Dylan Thomas, Leonard Cohen, and Gwen MacEwen. I began to read and respond to literature in a way I hadn't before in the works of Thomas Hardy, John Steinbeck, and Ernest Hemingway. One time, in the middle of the night, I awoke and heard a voice. It was my own voice. I wrote my first poem. It was an awakening. In the summer after grade twelve, at a local library I borrowed James Joyce's *A Portrait of the Artist as a Young Man*. What struck me about this book was its realistic yet poetic language, original imagery, and beautiful passages. This book described the life of the main character, Stephen Dedalus and his development as a writer. When I finished the book, I decided that I wanted to be a writer.

In the final year of high school, I read as much literature as possible: Milton, Austen, Yevtushenko, T.S. Eliot etc. I wrote my first book of poems "Pearls." After the first year at The University of Western Ontario, I decided to travel to Europe, to get out into the world and experience more. I lived in Northern Ireland during the beginning of the troubles. I lived in London, England working as a waiter, bookseller, and an usher at the Old Vic. I hitchhiked through France, Spain, Morocco, and Italy.

Later in Montreal I completed an MA in Creative Writing. My thesis became my third book of poems, *Blue Riders*. During my Ph.D. I was exposed to a wide range of authors and having to read and analyze their work in depth, made it possible to develop my writing style. I wanted to write poems that were structurally more complex, where the argument was more subtly integrated into the poem, where I could build images into networks naturally within the overall development of the poem. Reading the

English Romantic poets, and twentieth century American poets and Canadian poets helped me become more aware of the possibilities of the poem in my works. The poems I wrote then eventually found their way into my next poetry book, *Foreign National.*

You mentioned "artist's statement." I think that a central part of my aesthetics is expressed in my poem "Spoon." I wanted this poem to have a larger life of its own. Sometimes an ordinary object become more symbolic, almost allegorical. I want my poems to be unpredictable, do go in unexpected directions, to engage the reader intimately and take them to other places that they have never seen before – places with a more powerful sense of connection and significance. This is what I try to do in these poems. You try to write a poem that is almost inconceivable, but somehow you make it possible. I like this sense of development in a poem which is organic in nature, which has a unity, and an inevitable course. You find this in poets like Pablo Neruda, Octavio Paz, and Gaston Miron and in contemporary Canadian poets Don McKay and Brian Bartlett.

JF: Your parents met in 1945 in Holland, your mother Dutch, your Irish father in the RAF. In 1954 your family, moved to Canada. In the past sixty years you've established yourself as an important Canadian poet and Canadian poetry scholar. At the same time, you have written many memorable poems about your early life in Ireland and Holland, and the lives of your Irish and Dutch family members and ancestors. You seem to me to hold a special place in Canadian Literature as a Baby Boomer Canadian with very real ties to the rural societies of Ireland and Holland in the forties and fifties, to the shadows of World War II hovering over Europe. Could you discuss aspects of your identity as a "foreign national", as one who moves "beyond borders"?

LH: I have several times in my life when I felt like a "foreign national." My parents met just after the war. My father was Irish and in the Royal Air Force stationed at Valkenburg, Holland and he met my Dutch mother at a dance. Up until I was six, I spent time in Ireland and Holland. I went to kindergarten in Wassenaar, the place where my mother was from, for a several months and was able to learn Dutch. For a few years, I felt like an immigrant in Canada. Being a first-generation immigrant with ties to my parents' countries, you keep those ties. With Ireland it was the amusing stories of my father's growing up in Derry and working in Belfast. His stories were of meeting famous people of this time like the actor, Stan Laurel. My mother and her family often talked about the war so that it became part of my imagination, and this found its way into my poems. Many of my friends were Irish, German, and Italian and it was natural to share stories of our backgrounds.

Having parents coming from different countries, I had the pleasure of observing life through different linguistic lenses, so this motivated me to develop an interest in French language and literature. I moved to Montreal and later to Edmundston, New Brunswick. I have always in some way been living near borders, whether geographical, political, cultural, or linguistic. This was the case in Edmundston when I was living in a French city on the American border teaching at the Université de Moncton. I've found it rewarding to learn different languages, to be able read poets in their original languages.

JF: I'm struck by your enthusiasm for research and reflection on the village of Emery in which you grew up. Emery was a village swallowed up by suburban development in North York. Emery is your most documentarian poetry book to date, and unlike most of your poetry, which moves between the close and intimate and the faraway and wide, the focus in these collections is steadily microscopic. What do you make of your move from very old societies into a pioneer village? Why did Emery come to mean so much to you?

LH: I was nine years old when we moved to Emery and eighteen when we left, so these were very formative years. In 1957 part of the old community still existed, including the village, the church, the two-room schoolhouse, and many of the original farmhouses. We jumped in the haylofts in the barns and were chased off the land for stealing apples from the orchards. I went to school with the farmer's kids. Later when I attended Emery Collegiate Institute, I saw the old war monument and the bell from the two-room schoolhouse in the courtyard and I remembered where they had come from. It was all that was left of the community.

When thirty years later I was working on my PhD dissertation, I had a dream in which a farmer was leaning on a fence and calling out to me, "Come visit us, we have a history to tell you." A few years later at the League of Canadian Poets conference in Victoria College I was talking to James Reaney and his wife Colleen Thibaudeau. Her sister, Sheila Lambrinos surprisingly told me that she had written a booklet on Emery containing a history of its beginning at the time of John Graves Simcoe, a map with a list of farmers who lived there, and I recognized some of the names. Over the next three summers, I tracked down the farmers and interviewed them. One of the former inhabitants, Orrie Truman was a medic who had been through the Battle of El Alamein, through Sicily and all the way up to Pisa. He was responsible for having the bell and the monument transferred from the old Emery community to the high school.

JF: There is drama and dialogue/monologue in your poetry, your poems are often narrative in structure, and you've written fine prose poems. Why have all eight of your creative writing books been poetry? Have you considered writing drama, fiction, or creative non-fiction? Do you ever find poetry limiting or challenging as a form?

LH: Yes, I have published mostly poetry. At one time I was thinking about becoming a novelist. At the end of high school, I wrote a novel, and during the 1970s I wrote another one as well as short stories. I was not satisfied with these, so I never tried to publish them. I have also written non-fiction, a memoir about my Dutch family during the Second World War. A few years ago, I wrote a story about playing with the Edmundston Eskimos against NHL old timers such as Guy Lafleur, Gilbert Perreault and Gaston Gingras which was published in *The Windsor Review* several years ago. Maybe one day I will return to prose to write non-fiction and a novel.

JF: How does your painting intersect with your poetry? How long have you been painting? I find your painting much more abstract, expressionistic, surreal than your poetry. If I was assigned to find illustrations for your poetry, I might look at the "magic realism" of Atlantic Canadian artists Alex Colville and Christopher and Mary Pratt. Please comment.

LH: Those are intriguing comments. I've always been interested in painting since when I was seven, to see my Uncle Herman in his bed-room studio whereby using watercolours and tiny brushes he recreated canals, tulips, windmills of Holland—it was magic!

In 1976 I saw a film on contemporary American art featuring Jackson Pollock, Jasper Johns, Robert Rauschenberg which introduced me to abstract expressionism. I was fascinated by how many different strategies, approaches, techniques that the artists employed in these paintings—it exploded my whole conception of art. I wrote a poem called "Music in the Snow" in which I created different perspectives like images in an abstract painting. About ten years ago I noticed that there were more and more references to art in my poetry I was, in fact, expressing a desire to paint. In 2009 I decided to take a course with artist, Réjean

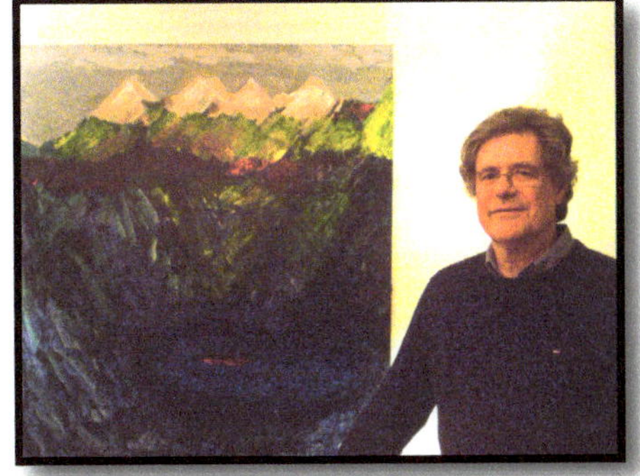

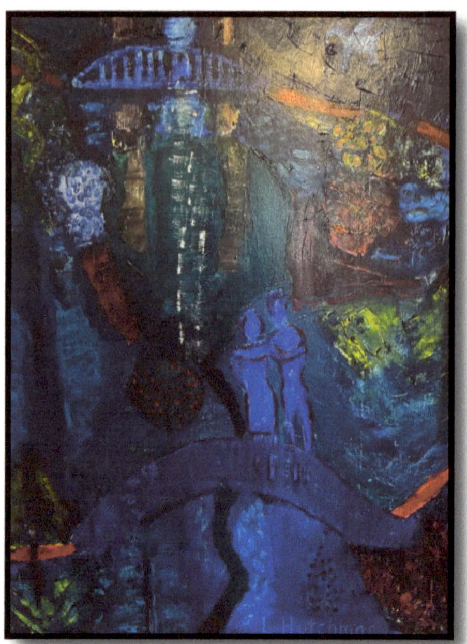

Meeting on the Bridge

Toussaint at the Université de Moncton. I painted scenes of my Irish early, scenes of Machu Picchu and Santiago, referring to the poetry of Pablo Neruda and a painting that I based on Rilke's *The Duino Elegies*. I never felt such freedom of expression. It was an exciting time. After several years and several art courses, I had a show at the Galerie Colline in Edmundston entitled "At the Border of Painting and Writing." There is something so immediate, physical, emotional, about the act of painting; I could "say" things that I couldn't in the same way in poems.

JF: You taught Canadian Literature and Creative Writing for many since years at the Université de Moncton. You have expressed a love of teaching. What effects have an adulthood spent teaching full-time had on your creative writing?

LH: That's a very broad question. I had the good fortune to be able to teach at a several universities for more than thirty-five years. I taught many different courses on authors such as Chaucer, Shakespeare, Milton, Wordsworth which gave me knowledge of the tradition of English literature. My favourite areas were the English Romantic poets, twentieth century American literature, and contemporary Canadian poetry. I liked the English romantic period because of the diversity of the poetry. I appreciated Wordsworth and Keats for their long lines, so finely structured and developed with such powerful, original imagery. I admired poems which have these qualities and I tried to develop them in my own work. Modern American poetry strongly attracted me because of its innovation and its variety, from the richly experimental poems of W.C. Williams to the powerful imagination of Wallace Stevens. I was also drawn to Elizabeth Bishop's beautifully wrought poems like "The Fish" and the poems of Galway Kinnell and Theodore Roethke. I explored Bly's deep-rooted imagery and "leaping poetry."

I enjoyed teaching literature. I was at home teaching Canadian poetry because I could tie many different things together. Teaching literature put me in the right frame of mind and gave me a certain constant fertility which made writing possible. Sometimes, the idea for poems would arrive during my trips to Fort Kent like the one about travelling in a spring snowstorm or another concerning Mahler.

JF: You've been deeply and fully engaged in the literary life of New Brunswick for over twenty years. From 2000 to 2008 you held executive positions, including President, of the Writers' Federation of New Brunswick. What do you see as some of the challenges and possible rewards of being a New Brunswick writer? What do you think you may have contributed to New Brunswick writing in your work with WFNB?

LH: In New Brunswick we are not close to the larger urban centres and the population is relatively small. Yet there has been a literary tradition beginning with Charles G.D. Roberts and Bliss Carman, Alden Nowlan, John Thompson and Travis Lane, and other excellent contemporary poets because there is an audience for literature. It has had important literary magazines *The Cormorant*, Alan Cooper's *Germination* and *The Fiddlehead*, the oldest literary magazine in Canada. There is a long tradition of poetry to Bliss Carman and Charles G.D. Roberts to Alden Nowlan here.

In my work with the Writers' Federation of New Brunswick, I wanted to try to have a greater involvement with the writers in the province, including the Acadian writers such as Léonard Forest, France Daigle, and Raymond Guy LeBlanc. I also wanted them to give readings, workshops, and to participate in the Alden Nowlan Literary Festival. Each year we gave a tribute to a different writer: Alden Nowlan, Fred Cogswell, Robert Gibbs to name a few.

In the WFNB I was working with a group of dedicated volunteers. We brought in Wesley McNair, the poet Laureate of Maine, Maggie Dominic from New York to the Alden Nowlan Festival, writers from Ontario, Quebec, and the other Maritime provinces such as Michael Winter, Michael Crummey, David Adams Richards, and Alistair MacLeod. We also opened the literary contests to the rest of the country.

JF: Your life in Edmundston and for a brief time in Fort Kent, Maine, exposed you to Madawaskayan and Acadian poets. You were a frequent participant in New Brunswick's annual "Salon du livre" in Edmundston, and you were Canadian poetry editor of the University of Maine at Fort Kent's literary journal *River Review / Revue Rivière*. Could you discuss your engagement in the local 'scene' and what import the literature of this region has?

LH: During my years in the Edmundston region, my connections with writers were mostly from Maine, Bill Willan, Paul Hedeen, the novelist, Cathie Pelletier and Wesley McNair. I attended lectures, readings at conferences at the Université of Maine at Fort Kent. In *the River Review, La Revue Rivière*, in which I was a Canadian editor, we published Canadian writers introducing them to an American public.   I presented a dossier of Acadian poets Gérald Leblanc, Rose Després, and Dyane Léger and Marc Arsenault. I also published interviews with Louis Dudek, Roo Borson, and James Reaney. The "Salon du livre" was an important annual book event in Edmundston that brought together French-speaking writers from New Brunswick, Quebec, Nova Scotia, and France. It was a pleasure to meet these writers and poets from other places.

JF: You have said that your favourite New Brunswick poet is Alden Nowlan and that "he had it all". You also admire greatly the late Fred Cogswell, whom you write movingly about in "Fred Cogswell" (*Reading the Water*), praising his strong farm boy's fingers "that have written so many books". You write, "I love how you translated this land". In 2000 you founded a large, perhaps even extravagant literary festival in honour of Alden Nowlan ("Bread and molasses"), which lasted for four years and featured readings, panel discussions, workshops and book launches by Atlantic Canada's most important poets. Can you talk about your work and accomplishments in relation to these two men?

LH: I heard Alden Nowlan read at Western when I was in my first year. Already, he had a reputation as being one of the best poets in Canada. He had such an incredible presence, a rich resonant voice which was a bit rough then because he was recovering from an operation throat cancer. His writing was honest, direct, witty, coming out of his own life with such power. I remember that he read poems "I, Icarus," and "In the Operating Room" from the book, *Bread, Wine and Salt*, as well as "The Bull Moose." The lines were deep and had such integrity they shook you. They were epigrammatic. When I was thinking of creating a literary festival in Fredericton with a group of dedicated volunteers, I chose to name it after him because he represented most what was valued in Maritime poetry, a poetry that was accessible to everyone.

Fred Cogswell was also a key figure in Maritime literature, an important man of letters who was known as a poet, professor, critic, editor, and publisher. The second Alden Nowlan Festival was a tribute to him. He published more than three hundred writers with the Fiddlehead Poetry Books and a number of these poets went on to become serious writers. I met him at the League AGM meetings where he often made insightful comments on controversial issues. I was impressed with his keen intelligence and his command of the English language. When I began to work with the WFNB, I became close friends with him and his wife, Adele. I visited him frequently at his house in Douglas. He was a great storyteller regaling us with tales about Bliss Carman. One concerned taking his ashes across the US border, implying that they might not be his ashes after all and about Alfred Bailey and other writers. Fred was also excellent translator of French poetry.

JF: It's frustrating to write poetry for a world that's much more interested in fiction and film. Why do you persist? You're a terrific reader of your poetry, you've done over 300 readings, and you have a YouTube following for your accurate and hilarious mimicry of Al Purdy. Please talk about poetry and performance. What are your thoughts about poetry's future?

LH: Reading is a performance and when I read, I try to be aware of the verbal qualities of the poem since poetry is also an oral art. There are many things to consider when reading a poem as in the tone and pacing, but you need to be careful not to over read or be too dramatic as Hamlet said in his advice to the actors. Poems have for me almost a musical score and each poem suggests how it should be read and poets must pay attention to what the poem is saying. I like the poem to be memorable, to express the character of the poet's voice and we can hear this in the recordings of W.B. Yeats, W.H. Auden, Dylan Thomas or in the Canadian poets Irving Layton, Al Purdy or Leonard Cohen, who turned some of his poems into songs. It must possess an almost indefinable haunting quality that stays with one after hearing the poem.

Poetry will always be with us because it's one of the most powerful expressions of capturing who we are. When we consider the change in poetry over the centuries and especially in the twentieth century, we can see how radically it has changed. Poetry is always changing in its evolution as the poets move toward new forms of expression, to bring it closer to experience of the human speaking voice, to extend the reaches of the human imagination.

JF: You are founder and co-editor of *Coastlines: The Poetry of Atlantic Canada* (2002). Please discuss the development of this anthology, the challenges, and the rewards. There is a very high-quality representation of the sixty fine modern and contemporary poets selected, At the same time reviewers have noted that there's not a tremendous amount of formal innovation in the poetry and that perhaps rural landscapes and cultures dominate at the expense of more urban poetry. Please comment.

LH: When I began teaching Maritime literature, I discovered that there was not a contemporary anthology of Atlantic poetry. I asked Ross Leckie at the University of New Brunswick if he would be interested in compiling an anthology of Atlantic poetry and he replied that he would and he suggested that Anne Compton from the University of New Brunswick, Saint John join us. Later we asked Robin McGrath from Newfoundland to be an editor since we were not as familiar with Newfoundland literature. It took us about three years to bring this anthology together. It was a challenging task since we had to read the books of every Atlantic poet that was published, and this is what took so much time. The various poets were delegated, and we got together for meetings on Sundays at the Arts lounge at UNB. There were many heated discussions coming from different aesthetic positions. I think we created an excellent anthology that was representative of the different regions and provinces of Atlantic Canada. You mentioned that critics found that there was not considerable innovation. Yet, I think that there was a lot of innovation in the poetry—for example in the work of Thompson, Sinclair, Domanski, Vaughan, and Steffler. Poets can be innovative in different ways. We simply chose what we thought was the best and the most representative poetry that was available in the Atlantic provinces a certain period.

JF: Your collection *Reading the Water* (Black Moss Press, 2008) follows the lead of the poet's sport-fishing father: "He had strategies that I could only imagine. . ." "A soldier on a subversive campaign . . ." "he chose the right fly, the appropriate angle / lassoing the line . . . reading the sounds, the

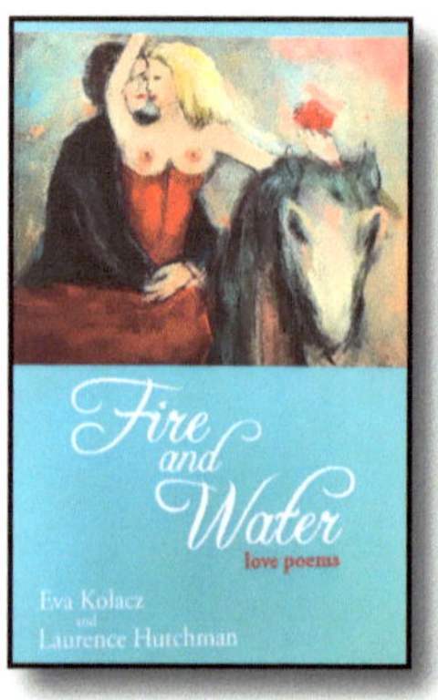

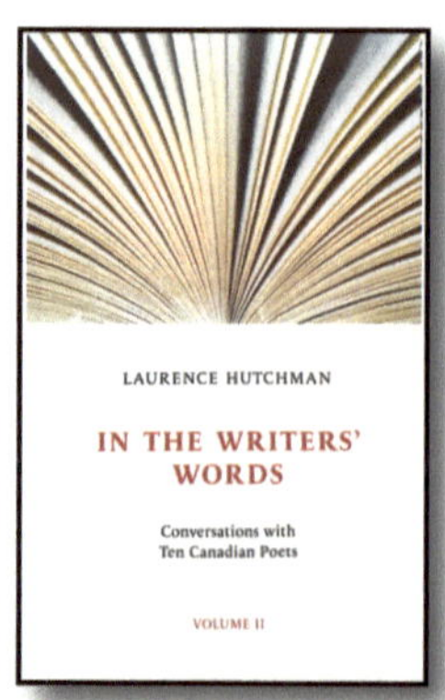

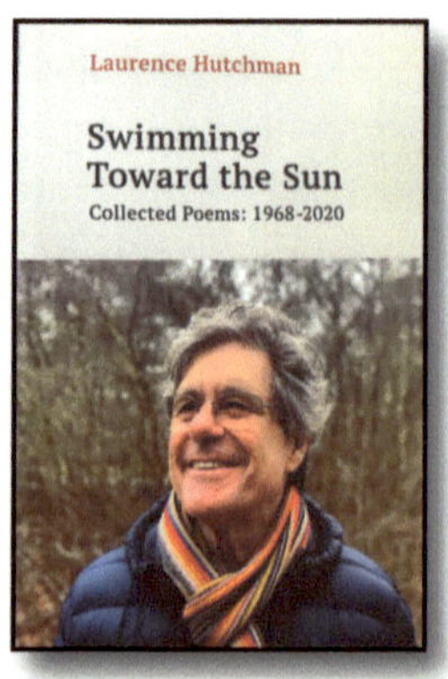

currents, the silences, / marks on a rippling dark page . . . / Timing was all." Reading the poems here I feel that the poet is moving slowly and powerfully, always in control of his voice and material. He grabs the reader in the first line of the first poem "Listening": "This morning, over the water / a voice in the light is calling, / Star of Venus, never brighter." Striking images pile on top of each other: pine trees "shrouded in their fuzzy coats," "The light, like blood, bevels on the water," gullets yodelling, "nightclub of the forest." The poet announces that he is discontent: "I leave this old self, / a snake skin, on the rock . . . ./ Forget your adolescence. / Give voice to your pain . . . / Shed your old skin . . . . / listen to the bristling music of birds, / the voices of morning."

The poet moves towards a refreshing, re-invigorated new life. In "Swimming Toward the Sun" the poet cannot stay in the cabin: "Others slept while I stepped / out. . . / I step down . . . / I think of those who died . . ./ I cry." Nature is full of musical life as the poet "swim(s) through." A great strength of the poems in this section is the internal rhyming that works beautifully. Can you talk about the poet's journey, his vigorous movement toward the light, the power of his voice?

LH: The two poems that you quote from "Listening" "Swimming Toward the Sun" are the first two poems from *Reading the Water*. In 2001 I was at Robert Bly's Great Mother Conference at Camp Kieve in Maine. Every morning I got up early and meditated before going for a swim. Upon awakening, you have a certain concentration in this liminal state, which allow you to be aware of the state of the water, rock, trees, animals and birds. Your mind is at one with the surroundings, but at the same time, there is the need for inner change, to "shed your old skin," awakening to the different possibilities that were around me. You can find in nature the purity of perception that you are searching for. In the second poem "Swimming Toward the Sun" there is this sense of moving toward a light, but first the necessity of going through some deeper changes an incorporating and understanding loss and gathering something from it. I feel liberated by water, but there is a certain strength that one gains by swimming as well as this feeling of unity at being with the elemental. I've written several poems about swimming in water, a kind of baptism, a cleansing of your body. This collection has a number of poems about rebirth, "Irish Spring," and," The Cave" for example.

JF: In your recent work *Personal Encounters*, the book can be seen as a tribute to artists, painters, sculptors, and poets. Can you speak about this book?

LH: Yes, this book concerns is called *Personal Encounters* because it deals the artists and writers that I have met and influenced me such as Irving Layton, Al Purdy, Leonard Cohen. It is also about artists such as Van Gogh, O'Keefe, and Rodin. Van Gogh had a strong influence on me when I was growing up. Yet the book is more than a tribute to them it is also about members of my family, my father, my Uncle Herman and my sister, Roberta. There are poems about my wife, the artist and poet, Eva Kolacz. The book is not only about encounters with people, but also objects like an ammonite or pencil, how we engage with them and how these encounters can change our perception of life.

February 2015

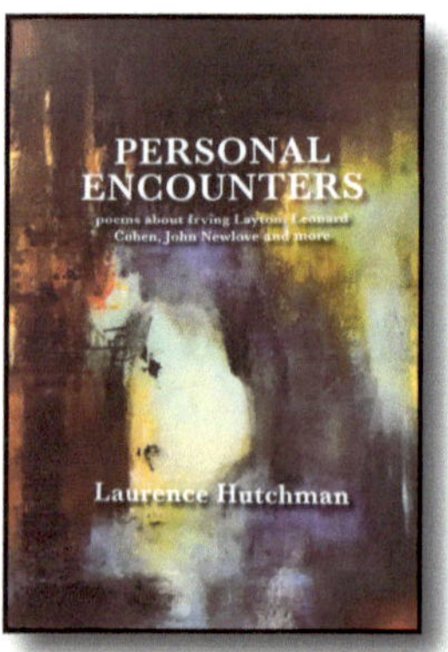

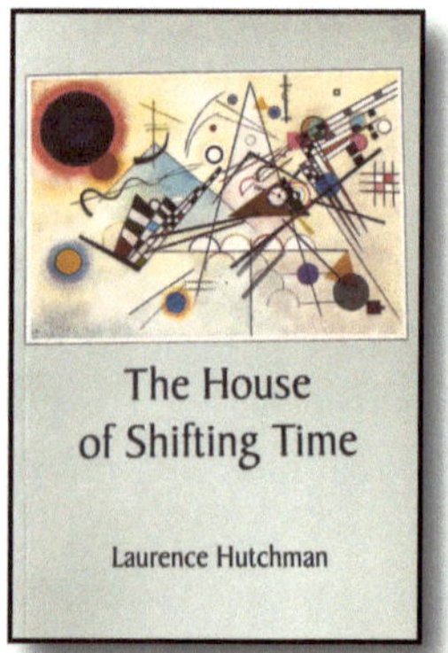

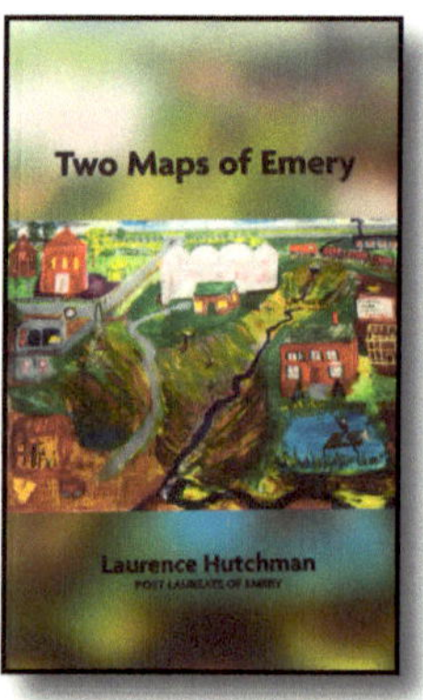

Interviewer, Janet Fraser, holds a Master's degree in English Literature from the University of Toronto. She specializes in Canadian literature and has written articles on AJM Smith and Canadian theosophy and many reviews of Canadian poetry. She is also the author of two poetry collections.

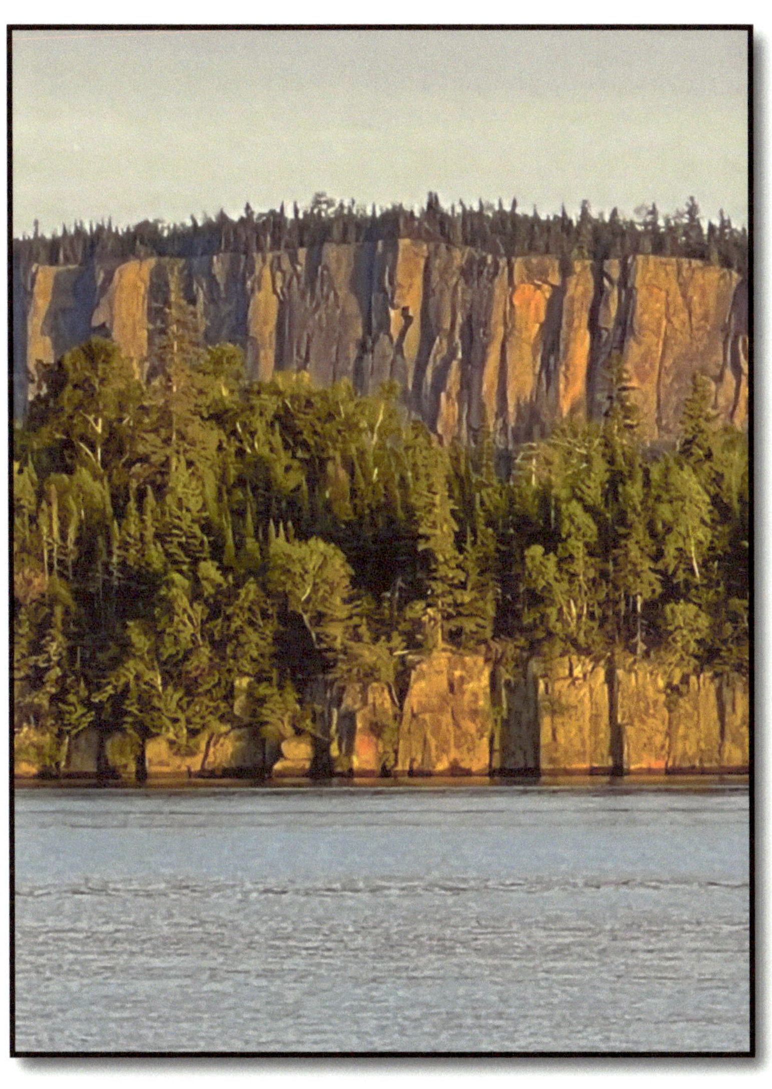

Thunderbay, Ontario
Ann Di Nardo

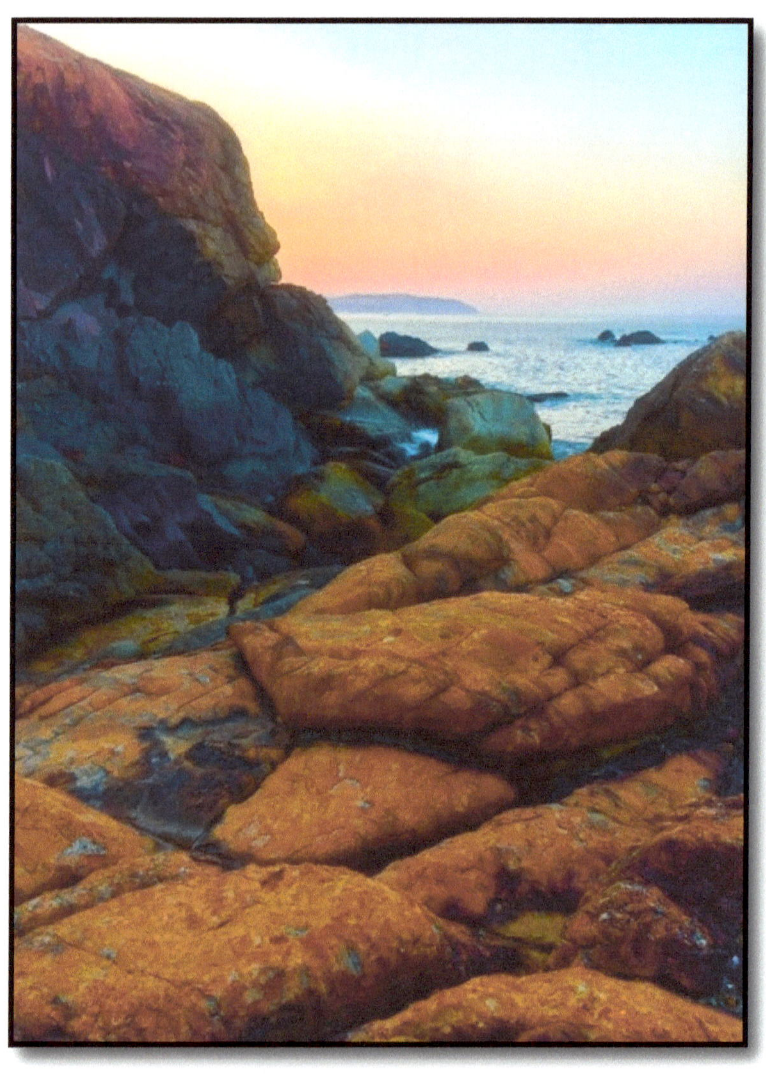

Goa, India
Ann Di Nardo

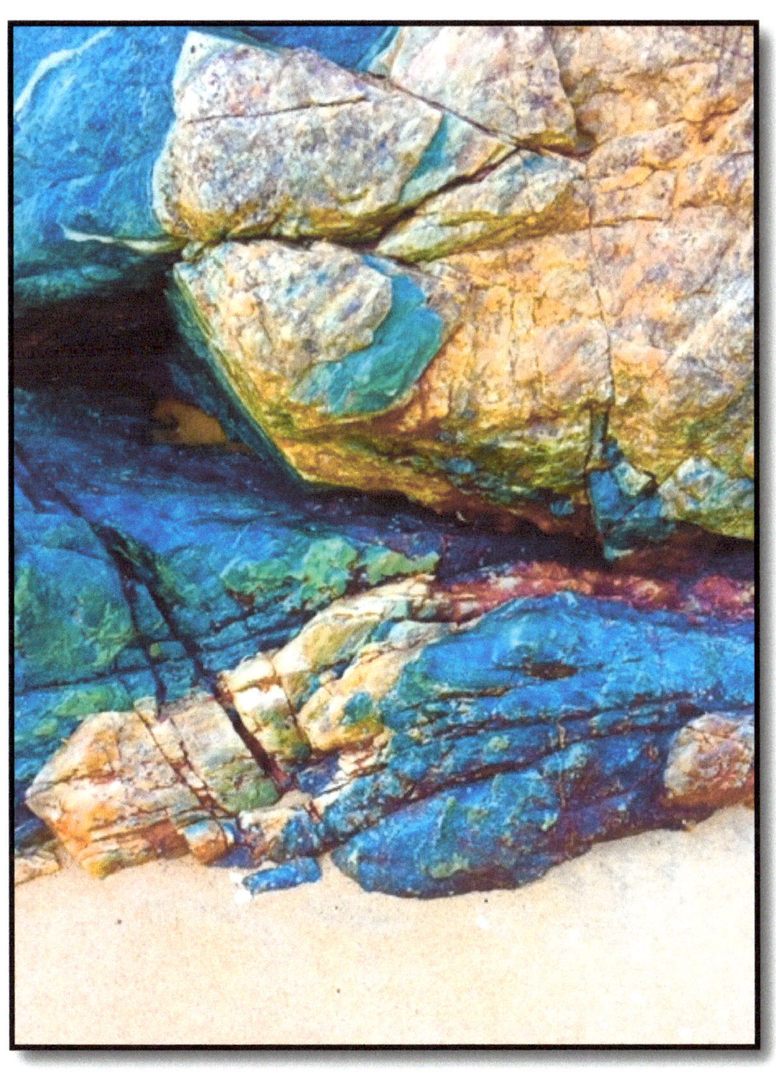

Goa, India
Ann Di Nardo

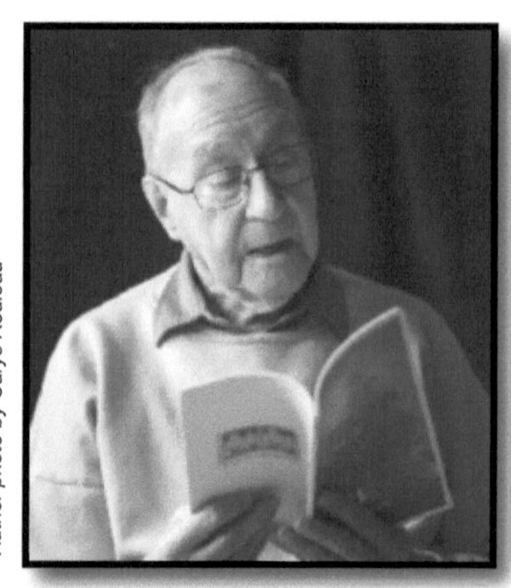

Stan White began life in Birmingham, England. He was an industrial photographer before coming to Canada in 1957 where he married and settled in Toronto working as a commercial and advertising photographer. In 1970 he joined Sheridan College as a teaching master and ran the studio for them for 20 years, teaching lighting and product illustration.

After he retired in the early 1990s, he continued with a life-long interest in stereo photography, photographing avidly in and around Brantford. These photographs are now in the local archives. In cooperation with the Photographic Historical Society of Canada, he set up a library of information on stereo photography now housed in the Art Gallery of Ontario.

Throughout his life, he has written non-fiction on various aspects of photography. In his 50s he began to write poetry and short stories. He has been published in local anthologies and has published several books of poetry, some in collaboration with other poets. As well he wrote a slim book on tabletop stereo imaging in 1970, Beyond the Third Dimension, published in the Netherlands and illustrated with ViewMaster reels.

These days, for relaxation, and in the hopes of slowing down the inevitable aging, he plays the musical saw and the Theremin, but keeps the windows closed.

A Review by Richard Grove

A copy of Stanley White's newest collection of short stories, **Short Tall Stories**, made its way into my infrequently idle hands. At this right moment with feet perched on an ataman I gazed past the Lake Ontario horizon and broke the spine on what ended up an intreaguing read. The cool squeak of my leather chair was quickly forgotten as I finished the first three-page story – "A Perfect Murder". No need for a spoiler alert, you can read the full story below.

One captivating short story after another led me to "Kafka's Great-Great-Great-Grandson". I have read enough of Kafka's work over the years that the title peeked my interest. The previous stories suggested I would not be let down. I will let you read the full story from his book but here is a teaser:

So the helping of broccoli was not altogether a surprise. The surprise was that I ate it. My wife tends to take offence if I don't eat everything she puts before me. I told her I would much rather suffer the dreaded disease that it was supposed to head off than eat the awful stuff.
The incident went completely out of my mind until several weeks later when I felt a slight irritation on the fleshy part of the inside of my left arm, about three inches down from where the nurse sticks the needle in to draw blood. There were five, minute dots of color. They looked, for all the world, like paint splatters. You know the kind—when the bristles of a paint brush flick and stipple your hand with perfectly round dots the color of the paint. These were green. I tried to scrape them off with my thumbnail. I tried soap. I tried pumice. But whatever they were, they were not going to come off easily. So I forgot about them, figuring they would probably go away by themselves. A day or two later I had cause to notice them again. The dots were now raised above the skin. They looked like green Braille. You might guess, whenever I was by myself, I examined them— sometimes a dozen times a day. Over the next several weeks I watched the dots develop into stalks and the ends of the stalks blossom into dark, vegetable-green blooms. I nibbled an end. It was unmistakably broccoli.

Stanley White's stories are short and will be a delightful gap-filler while you are waiting in the car for your wife to pick up broccoli for dinner. Don't snooze between stories. They might just make their way into a napping nightmare. This is what Richard Van Holst, author, copyeditor and book reviewer had to say about this original and inventive book.

Each of the short stories of Stanley J. White is set in a deftly created world which is both achingly real and startlingly imaginative. Here you will find everything from psychological drama and bittersweet human interest stories to murder mysteries and chilling tales of the paranormal and the post-apocalyptic, lightened now and again

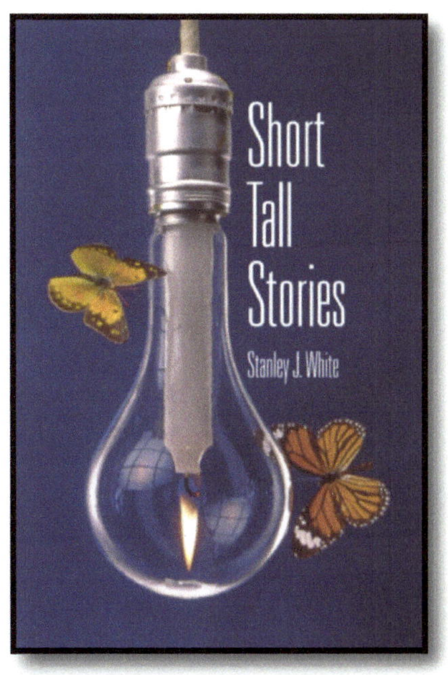

by a tour de farce which will have you chortling with glee. Explore exotic landscapes and secret hideouts, ponder the lofty aspirations of the lowly goldfish or musician, deplore the plight of the marginalized, tremble for those who teeter on the brink of insanity or despair, be astounded at the insights of an eccentric muse, and marvel at daredevils and pranksters who use all the wit and skill at their disposal to make the most of awkward situations. In short, these stories, crafted over a span of four decades, will delight you with their humour, touch you with their pathos, and enrich you with their observations on the human experience.

Beyond the Third Demention Press
ISBN – 978-0-9789463-3-6

A Perfect Murder *by Stanley White*

That he was a senior, whose criminal past concealed only an occasional ticket for speeding, and that he had led close to a blameless life and was highly respected in his church circle, gave his need even more urgency. For no apparent reason, and out of the blue, he found in late middle-age he was possessed with the urge to kill somebody. Perhaps it was because after his wife died he lived alone, and life was mind-bogglingly monotonous

He had watched TV programs in which killers, thinking they had "got away with it" found they had been tripped up by some unlikely event, some quirk of coincidence, somebody somewhere had noticed a car number plate, or some facet of forensic science had been overlooked. It was a challenge, but notwithstanding, he felt confident that with care he could commit the perfect murder. Clearly, he would have to avoid making even one tiny error that could put the police onto his track. The trick was not to leave anything to coincidence.

He would avoid firearms—they were noisy and too easily traced. A fluke gave him an opportunity for an alternative. On one of his drives, he stopped for lunch in a small town where there was an outdoor flea market… a few tables, and some vendors selling out of the trunks of their cars. One seller had a small modern crossbow, the kind used for hunting that fired a short, metal arrow called a bolt. It was exactly the tool for the job. It was a cash sale and there were no indoor store cameras there to record him.

Cars also were too easily traced, so he decided to use a bicycle for transport. There would be no obvious motive for his killing since he would choose a complete stranger. He would call him "the Dark Stranger".

On the evening of a fine day, he drove to a nearby town, leaving his car parked on the main street's free parking zone, and took off into the countryside on his bicycle.

He eventually came across a man walking along one of the smaller side roads. This man, he decided, would be "the Dark Stranger". Cycling past him, he rounded a bend until he was out of sight. Taking the bike with him over a gate and finding a gap in the hedge, with crossbow loaded, he waited for his victim. There were no dwellings in the area from which he might be observed and the road was empty in both directions. It proved an easy aim with his laser sight. At some twenty or so feet, the silent bolt found its mark. Conveniently, the man fell into the ditch at the side of the road. His body might not be discovered for days. Having achieved his objective without problems, he cycled back to his car. He then drove back to his home town where he stopped at a local pub, got stinking drunk, gave his car keys to the barman and took a taxi home. If necessary, he was sure the barman and the cab driver would remember him.

He had been wearing gloves throughout, and he spent the next several days shredding the clothes he had worn, including the shoes. He disassembled the crossbow and the bicycle so that everything was in tiny fragments, which he deposited in rivers, ponds, garbage bins miles from his home town, until everything to do with the murder had been distributed in a thousand places. He even resisted the temptation to follow the subsequent events, police announcements etc. as they pertained to the crime, feeling it might look suspicious if he took unusual interest. He was convinced he had committed the perfect crime.

*   *   *

Several weeks passed before the bombshell… he learned his son had been charged with murder. He was floored to find the man his son was charged with murdering was his "Dark Stranger". It ultimately turned out that the two men had an association, and that there was great rancor between them. In fact, they had recently fought, and the police were brought in. On the night of the murder, they were scheduled to meet each other. If that wasn't enough to arouse suspicion, his son also belonged to a local hunting club in which they sometimes used crossbows. The police figured his motive was that the man had been playing around with his wife.

To save his son he confessed, but the police didn't believe him. Show us some proof, they said, but of course he couldn't, since all was beyond recovery. So thorough had he been that even he couldn't produce a shred of evidence that he had committed the crime. It was obviously a case of a father trying to take the blame for his son's sins.

The evidence against his son was purely circumstantial but it was so prolific and damaging that it took the jury just four hours to find him guilty.

He was sentenced to 25 to life.

Pre-History Forest of Madawaska

Deep, deep in the pre-history forest of Madawaska
fading shadows crisscross the pine-needle-carpeted woodland
of infinity where life whispers the ancient enigma of eternity.
Trees rise and trees fall in the silence
of the phase-less primeval quietude
where timeless years inch into an everlasting yesterday.

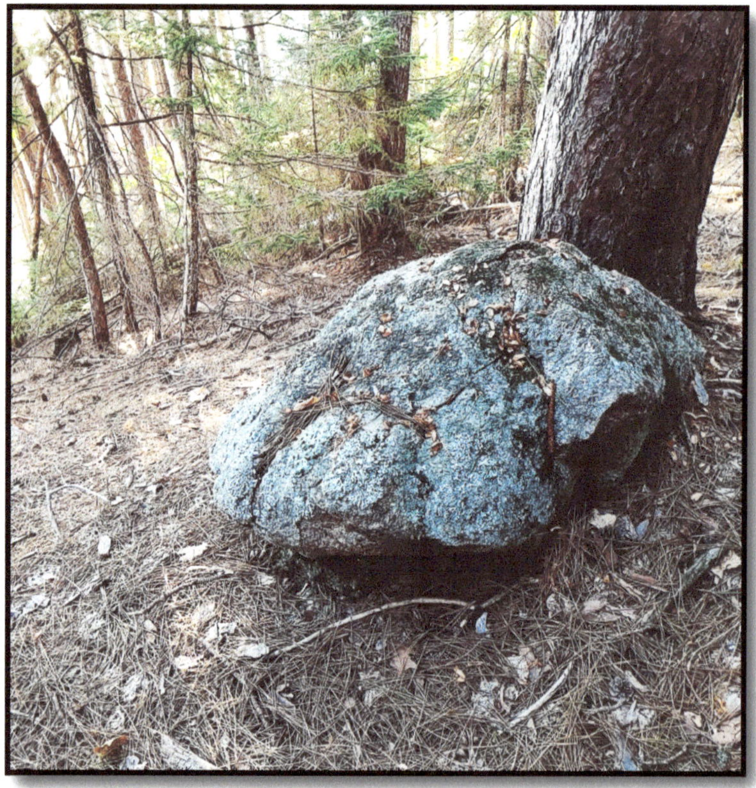

Madawaska, Ontario
Richard Marvin Tiberius Grove

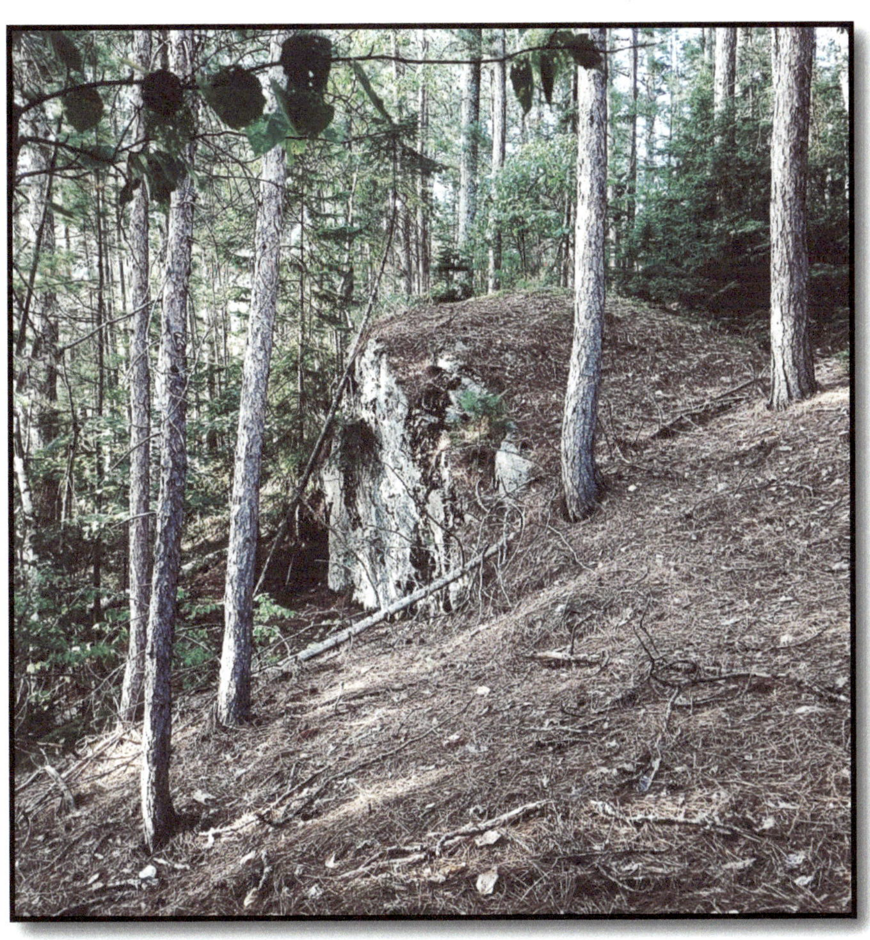

Madawaska, Ontario
Richard Marvin Tiberius Grove

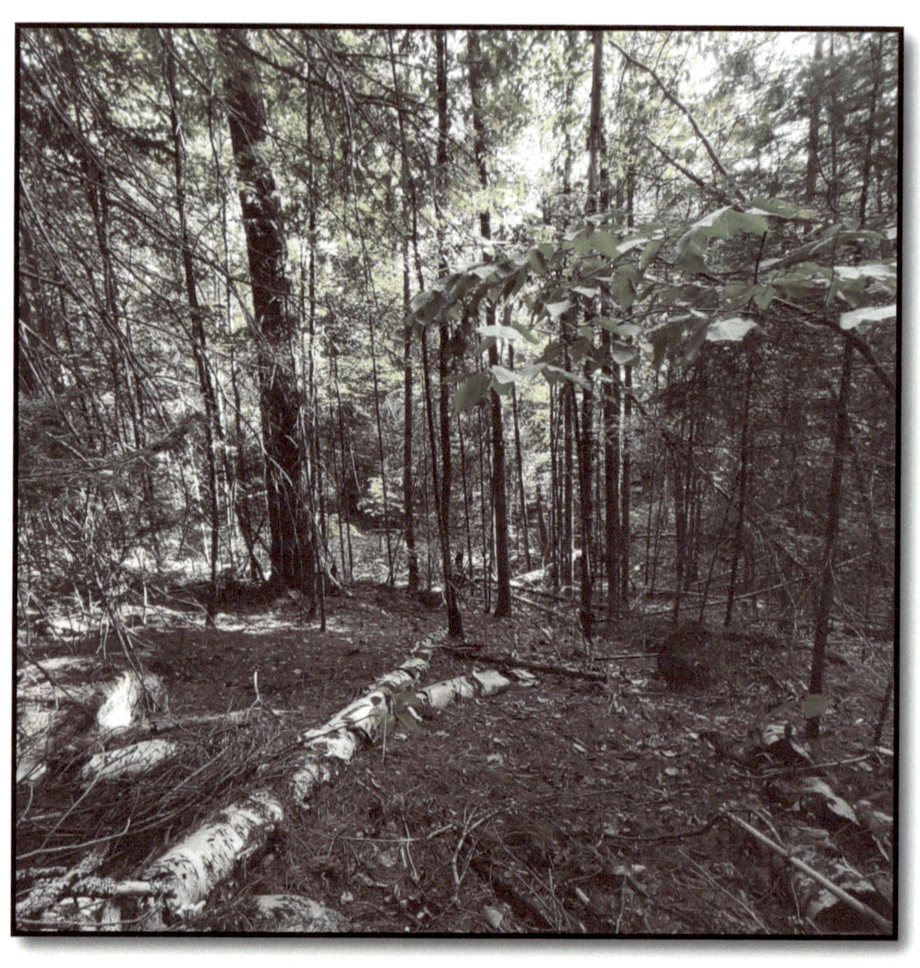

Madawaska, Ontario
Richard Marvin Tiberius Grove

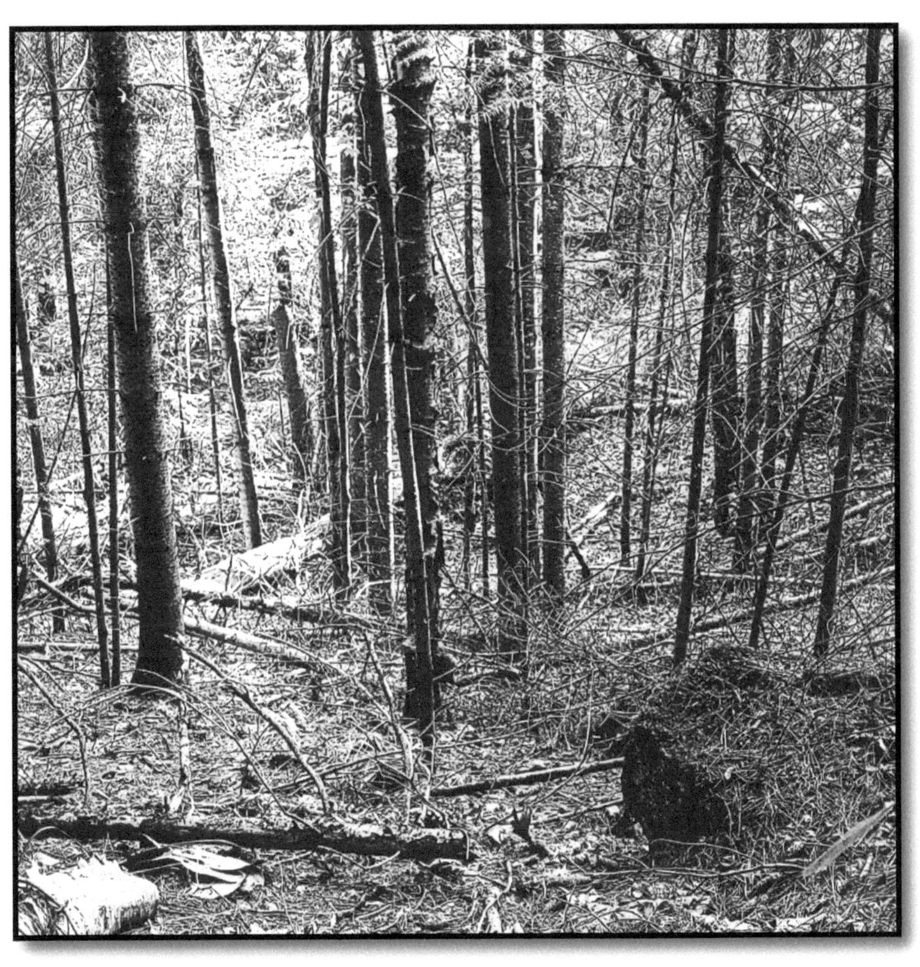

Madawaska, Ontario
Richard Marvin Tiberius Grove

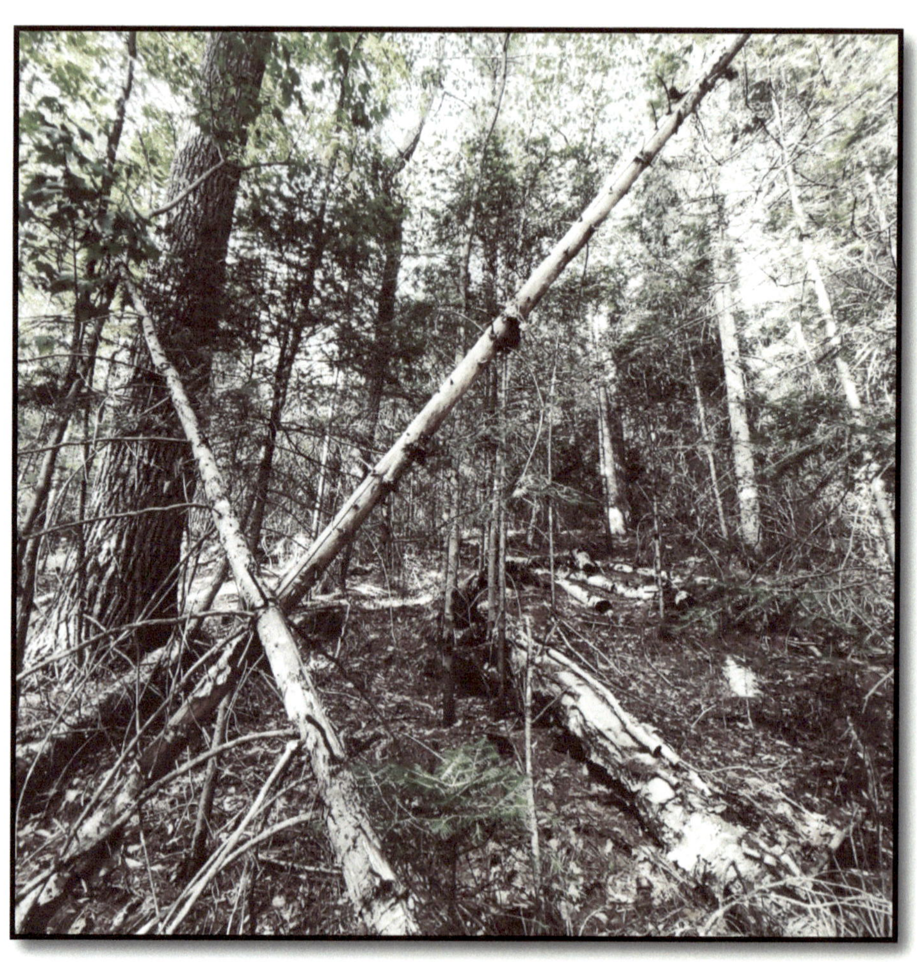

Madawaska, Ontario
Richard Marvin Tiberius Grove

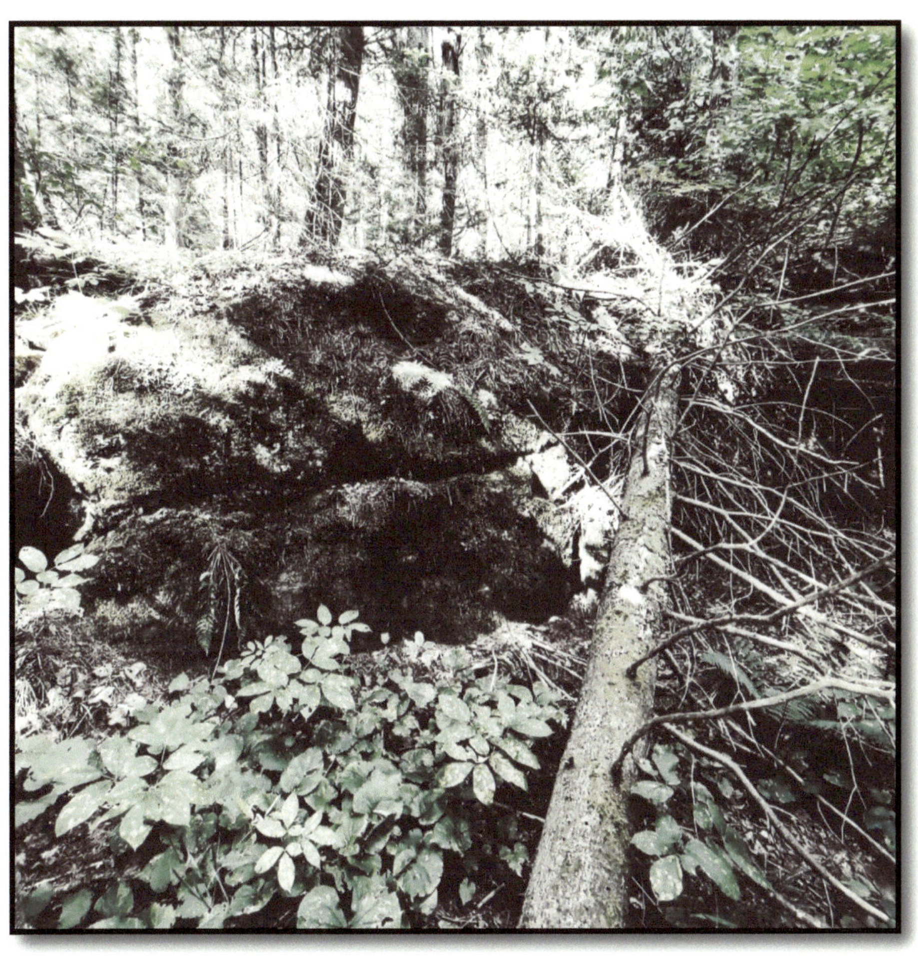

Madawaska, Ontario
Richard Marvin Tiberius Grove